SCHOLASTIC ATLAS OF OCEANS

SCHOLASTIC REFERENCE

Library of Congress Cataloging-in-Publication Data available

0-439-56128-0

10 9 8 7 6 5 4 3 2   04 05 06 07 08

Printed in the U.S.A.
First printing, September 2004

Scholastic Atlas of Oceans was created and produced by:

QA International
329, rue de la Commune Ouest, 3e étage
Montréal (Québec) H2Y 2E1 Canada
T 514.499.3000   F 514.499.3010
www.qa-international.com

Editorial Director
Caroline Fortin

Editor in Chief
Martine Podesto

Editor
Marie-Anne Legault

Writer
Donna Vekteris

Graphic Designer
Josée Noiseux

Layout
Jean-François Nault

Art Director
Anouk Noël

Illustrators
Carl Pelletier   Raymond Martin
Rielle Lévesque   Claude Thivierge
Danielle Lemay   François Escalmel
Jocelyn Gardner   Marie-Andrée Lemieux

Research and Photo Acquisition
Nathalie Gignac
Fernand Chevalot

Proofreading
Veronica Schami Editorial Services

Oceanographer
Serge Lepage

Page 8, marine iguana: Eric and David Hosking/CORBIS/Magmaphoto.com Page 9,
Kilauea volcano: James A. Sugar/CORBIS/Magmaphoto.com • giant tortoise: Correl Cd rom •
moai: Wolfgang Kaehler/CORBIS/Magmaphoto.com Page 11, Iceland: Karl Grönvold •
pirate: The Richard T. Rosenthal Collection. • Tristan da Cunha: David Robinson Page 12,
dhow: Nick Smyth; Cordaiy Photo Library Ltd.CORBIS/Magmaphoto.com Page 13, coelacanth:
Juergen Schauer/JAGO-Team • lemur: Dr. Anthony R. Picciolo, NOAA NODC • Piton de la
Fournaise: Gallo Images/CORBIS/Magmaphoto.com Page 16, treasure: Richard T. Nowitz
/CORBIS/Magmaphoto.com Page 17, Mediterranean Sea: AFP/CORBIS/Magmaphoto.com •
Aral Sea: Shepard Sherbell/CORBIS SABA/Magmaphoto.com • South China Sea: GeoStock
/Getty Images • Dead Sea: Ricki Rosen/CORBIS SABA/Magmaphoto.com Page 27, Aleutian
Islands: Angus Wilson Page 35, Caribbean Sea: Bob Krist/CORBIS/Magmaphoto.com Page 55,
bathysphere: Ralph White/CORBIS/Magmaphoto.com Page 59, Alvin: ©R. Catanach, Woods
Hole Oceanographic Institution Page 60, narwhal: Flip Nicklin/Minden Pictures • walrus:
NOAA NODC Page 61, polar bear: D. Robert & Lorri Franz /CORBIS /Magmaphoto.com Page 66,
sea otter: Galen Rowell/CORBIS/Magmaphoto.com Page 67, sea grass: William Boyce/CORBIS
/Magmaphoto.com Page 76, Titanic: Ralph White/CORBIS/Magmaphoto.com Page 78, salt flat:
James Marshall/CORBIS/Magmaphoto.com Page 79, marine farming: Hans Georg Roth/CORBIS
/Magmaphoto.com • seaweed: Michael S. Lewis/CORBIS/Magmaphoto.com Page 80, nodule:
JAMSTEC • sponge: Dave G. Houser/CORBIS/Magmaphoto.com Page 81, soft coral: J.G.
Harmelin, Centre d'Océanologie de Marseille, France Page 83, wind turbine: Paul A. Souders
/CORBIS/Magmaphoto.com Page 87, great auk: Academy of Natural Sciences of Philadelphia
/CORBIS /Magmaphoto.com • coral bleaching: Stephen Frink/CORBIS/Magmaphoto.com

Conversion chart

Metric	U.S.	
1 cm	0.4	in.
1 m	3.28	ft
1 km	0.62	mile
10 km	6.21	miles
100 km	62.14	miles

Key to abbreviations

mm	=	millimeter
m	=	meter
sq km	=	square kilometer
in.	=	inch
mph	=	mile per hour
cm	=	centimeter
km	=	kilometer
km/h	=	kilometer per hour
ft	=	foot
lb	=	pound

Contents

Portrait of the oceans

Every sea and ocean on our planet has a unique shape and character. The Pacific Ocean always seems stormy, while the Atlantic buzzes with shipping traffic. The Indian Ocean is warm, while the polar oceans remain ice-cold. Some oceans and seas appear to be endless, while others have visible land borders.

Of land and water

We may live on land, but we cannot survive without the ocean. The water covering most of our planet helps create the air we breathe. Millions of tiny plants that live in the ocean produce the precious gas in the air, which we call oxygen. The ocean also works to keep our climate comfortable. Its cold and warm currents travel the globe, heating and cooling entire countries. Huge amounts of water on its surface are constantly evaporating, then falling as rain or snow over other parts of the world. Acting like a giant heat reservoir, the ocean even collects the Sun's excess rays, preventing the Tropics from burning up!

Deep beneath the ocean's surface is a hidden universe. This mysterious world has its own towering mountains, deep valleys, and even exploding volcanoes. It is also home to an amazing variety of animals. Rising up from the ocean floor, islands and continents divide the ocean into five different oceans as well as several dozen seas.

DIVIDING THE WORLD'S OCEAN

Even though they are geographically separated into five distinct areas, the world's oceans are really one single, gigantic body of water. The Pacific has the biggest share, covering almost half the earth.

Arctic: 4%

Atlantic: 23%

Pacific: 46%

Indian: 21%

Southern: 6%

A long-distance record

The record holder for the longest mountain range in the world is the Mid-Oceanic Ridge. This underwater chain of mountains runs through nearly all the oceans of our planet. Stretching for an incredible 40,000 miles (64,372 km), the Mid-Oceanic Ridge is four times longer than the Andes, the Rockies, and the Himalayas put together!

When is an ocean a sea?

A sea is a fragment or piece of ocean that is either partially or entirely surrounded by land. Some of the world's seas are connected to the ocean by short water passageways called straits.

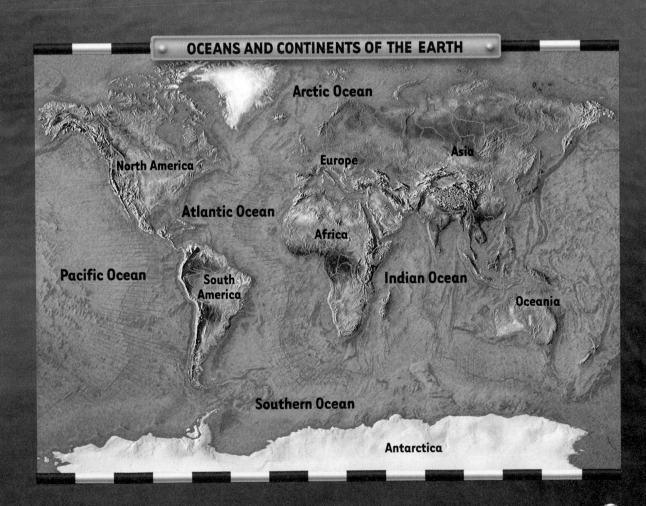

OCEANS AND CONTINENTS OF THE EARTH

Arctic Ocean

North America

Europe

Asia

Atlantic Ocean

Africa

Pacific Ocean

South America

Indian Ocean

Oceania

Southern Ocean

Antarctica

A misnamed ocean

When the Portuguese navigator Magellan came upon the vast ocean lying between Asia, America, and Oceania in 1520, he found it so calm that he named it the "Pacific," which means peaceful or quiet. But with 300 active volcanoes, fearsome tropical storms, powerful earthquakes, and the highest waves in the world, the Pacific is actually the most violent of all the oceans! At an average of about 13,000 feet (4,000 m) below sea level, the floor of the Pacific presents an uneven landscape. It is broken up by very deep trenches and crisscrossed by long chains of mountains. The peaks of the tallest mountains reach all the way up to the surface, forming countless islands and islets.

The Pacific Ocean is by far the largest of the oceans. It contains half of all the water on the planet and covers almost a third of Earth's surface. The Pacific's different currents and climates support an amazing variety of marine life, from the gigantic blue whale of the cold North Pacific to the colorful coral in the warm tropical waters of Australia's Great Barrier Reef.

A bold colonization

In spite of their isolation, it didn't take long for the Pacific islands to attract new life. Plant seeds were carried to the islands in the claws of birds, blown by winds, or pushed by ocean currents. Some reptiles arrived by sea, floating on tree branches, coconuts, or bits of wreckage. Insects were transported long distances by tropical storms. The first humans sailed here from southeast Asia on wooden sailboats. These daring navigators watched the shapes of the waves and the flight patterns of birds to guide them from one island to the next.

Marine iguana, Galápagos Islands

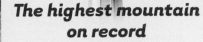

Kilauea volcano on Hawaii

The islands of Hawaii form America's 50th state. Made up of some 132 islands, this paradise for surfers and divers is also a gold mine for scientists who study volcanoes. To the south lies Kilauea, which can be safely observed by them as well as by the public, even though it is one of the most active volcanoes in the world. Lava has been flowing out of Kilauea nonstop since 1983!

The highest mountain on record

The largest volcano in the world is Mauna Kea on Hawaii's biggest island. Its peak rises 13,796 ft (4,205 m) above sea level. However, if one adds to this the other 16,400 ft (5,000 m) hidden underwater, Mauna Kea stands almost 30,000 ft (9,200 m) high, beating Mount Everest by 1,150 ft (350 m)!

North America

Hawaii

Giant tortoise of the Galápagos Islands

Made up of 13 islands and 17 islets, the Galápagos Islands are home to some unusual plants and animals found nowhere else in the world. Marine iguanas, the only known aquatic lizards, live on its shores along with giant tortoises, some of which are more than 150 years old!

Papua New Guinea

Solomon Islands

Galápagos Islands

Pacific Ocean

South America

Vanuatu

Fiji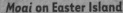

New Caledonia

Easter Island

Australia

Oceania

New Zealand

Moai on Easter Island

When the Dutch navigator Roggeveen discovered an island on Easter Day in 1722, he came across some giant, mysterious statues carved out of volcanic rock. Very little is known about the civilization that put up the statues on Easter Island, and history experts are still searching for clues. The tallest of these 887 stone figures, or *moai*, is 70 feet (21 m) tall (the height of a seven-story building).

Very busy waters

The Atlantic Ocean takes its name from Atlantis, a mythical civilization that is said to have disappeared beneath the waves long ago. Half the size of the Pacific Ocean, the Atlantic is the world's second-largest ocean, forming a gigantic "S" between Europe, Africa, and North and South America. The Atlantic has very few islands, yet there is plenty going on beneath its lifeless-looking surface. Swimming in its waters are large schools of cod, herring, sardines, hake, and other fishes. The millions of tons of fishes caught in the Atlantic each year make it one of the richest fishing zones in the world. The Atlantic sees a great deal of sea traffic. A nonstop stream of fishing boats, oil tankers, cargo ships, and ocean liners make its shipping lanes look like a giant water freeway.

Between the Old World and the New
For hundreds of years, Europeans were unaware of the continents that lay on the other side of the Atlantic. Among the first people to journey to North America were the Vikings, around the year 1000. Viking ships (also called longships) were large, open boats with oars and square sails. Christopher Columbus's discovery of the continent in 1492 led to a new era of exploration and trade. Over the next several hundred years, millions of Europeans in search of a better life would emigrate to the New World on large ships. Today, cargo ships carrying goods far outnumber the passenger boats sailing in and out of North America's harbors.

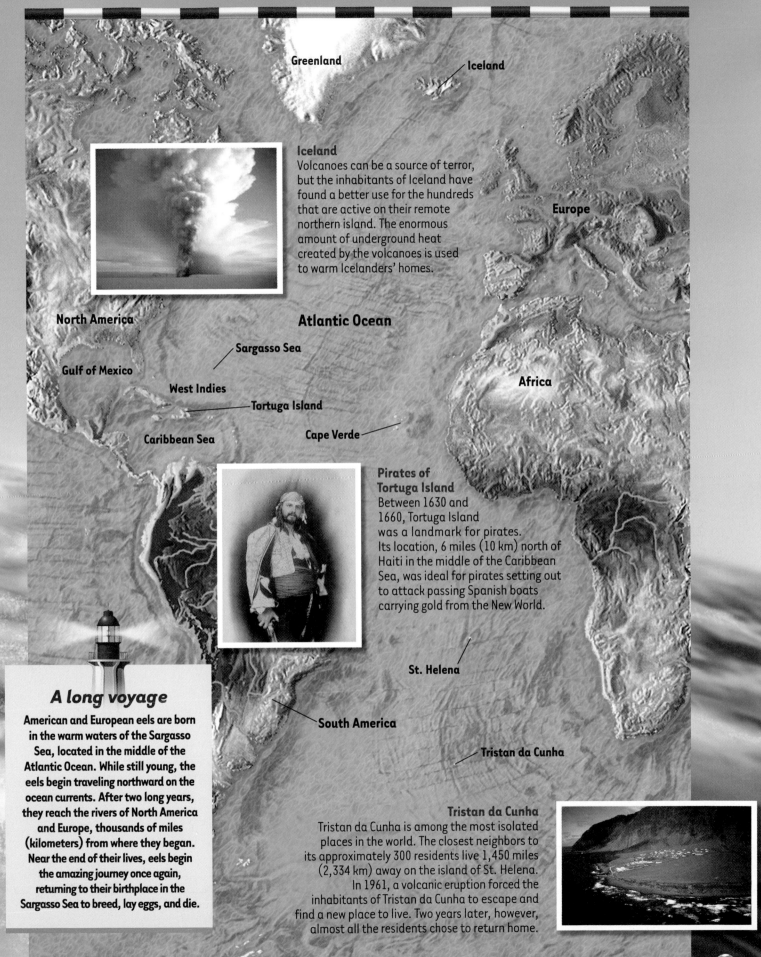

Greenland

Iceland

Iceland
Volcanoes can be a source of terror, but the inhabitants of Iceland have found a better use for the hundreds that are active on their remote northern island. The enormous amount of underground heat created by the volcanoes is used to warm Icelanders' homes.

Europe

North America

Atlantic Ocean

Sargasso Sea

Gulf of Mexico

West Indies

Africa

Tortuga Island

Caribbean Sea

Cape Verde

Pirates of Tortuga Island
Between 1630 and 1660, Tortuga Island was a landmark for pirates. Its location, 6 miles (10 km) north of Haiti in the middle of the Caribbean Sea, was ideal for pirates setting out to attack passing Spanish boats carrying gold from the New World.

St. Helena

A long voyage
American and European eels are born in the warm waters of the Sargasso Sea, located in the middle of the Atlantic Ocean. While still young, the eels begin traveling northward on the ocean currents. After two long years, they reach the rivers of North America and Europe, thousands of miles (kilometers) from where they began. Near the end of their lives, eels begin the amazing journey once again, returning to their birthplace in the Sargasso Sea to breed, lay eggs, and die.

South America

Tristan da Cunha

Tristan da Cunha
Tristan da Cunha is among the most isolated places in the world. The closest neighbors to its approximately 300 residents live 1,450 miles (2,334 km) away on the island of St. Helena. In 1961, a volcanic eruption forced the inhabitants of Tristan da Cunha to escape and find a new place to live. Two years later, however, almost all the residents chose to return home.

Tropical comfort

Lying between Africa and Oceania, the Indian Ocean takes its name from India, one of the countries it borders. As the third-largest ocean, it enjoys a tropical climate that makes its waters the warmest in the world. The Indian Ocean is also influenced by a unique phenomenon called the monsoon. This is a wind that blows one way during the dry season and the opposite way during the rainy season, causing the ocean's currents to reverse their direction twice a year. This exotic ocean is home to some heavenly landscapes: islands surrounded by white sand beaches, turquoise lagoons ringed with multicolored coral, and forests of mangrove trees, whose long roots grow below the water. The Indian Ocean features unique and spectacular animals, such as clown fish, butterfly fish, and parrot fish—brilliantly colored creatures that swim among the coral.

Careful, it's hot!

The Persian Gulf and the Red Sea, located in the Indian Ocean, contain the warmest waters in the world. Surface temperatures in the Persian Gulf in summertime can reach 100°F (38°C)—as warm as a hot tub! Volcanic activity at the bottom of the Red Sea raises the temperature of its waters to as high as 133°F (56°C) at 6,560 ft (2,000 m) below the surface—enough to cause third-degree burns to humans in just a few seconds!

Wind in the sails

Dhows are elegant boats that have been sailing the Indian Ocean for thousands of years. African, Arab, and Indian sailors have long used these boats in their trade with one another, taking advantage of the reversing direction of the monsoon winds. When winds and currents were traveling westward, Indian merchants would set sail for the Middle East and Africa, their dhows filled with wood, rice, and spices. The next season, when winds and currents changed direction, Africans would head for the Middle East and India, carrying gold, elephant ivory, and slaves. Traditional dhows are still found sailing the Indian Ocean today.

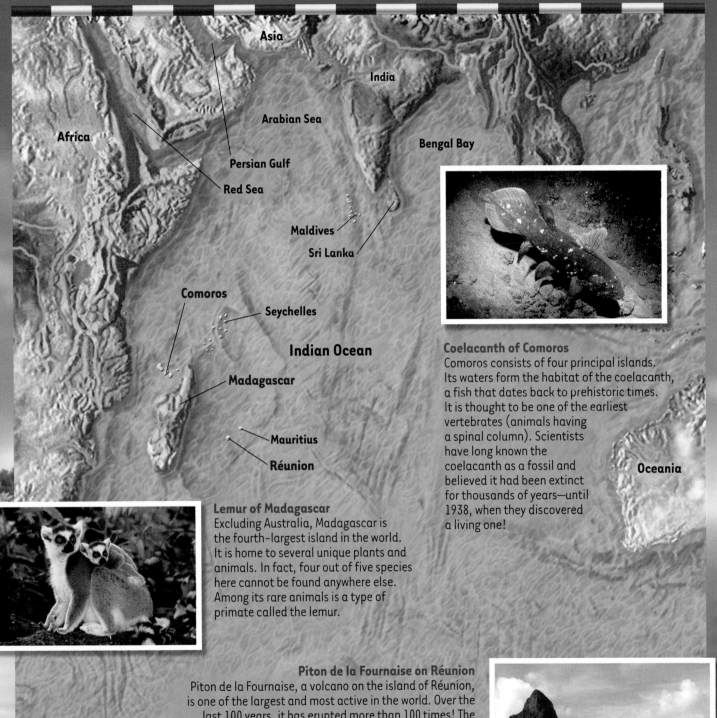

Asia

India

Arabian Sea

Africa

Bengal Bay

Persian Gulf

Red Sea

Maldives

Sri Lanka

Comoros

Seychelles

Indian Ocean

Madagascar

Mauritius

Réunion

Oceania

Coelacanth of Comoros
Comoros consists of four principal islands. Its waters form the habitat of the coelacanth, a fish that dates back to prehistoric times. It is thought to be one of the earliest vertebrates (animals having a spinal column). Scientists have long known the coelacanth as a fossil and believed it had been extinct for thousands of years—until 1938, when they discovered a living one!

Lemur of Madagascar
Excluding Australia, Madagascar is the fourth-largest island in the world. It is home to several unique plants and animals. In fact, four out of five species here cannot be found anywhere else. Among its rare animals is a type of primate called the lemur.

Piton de la Fournaise on Réunion
Piton de la Fournaise, a volcano on the island of Réunion, is one of the largest and most active in the world. Over the last 100 years, it has erupted more than 100 times! The volcano's abundant lava often flows down to the ocean, enlarging the island every time there is an eruption.

The frozen oceans

Spread out over the coldest parts of the globe are two extraordinary oceans: the Arctic at the North Pole and the Southern at the South Pole. With frigid temperatures rarely rising above 32°F (0°C), violent winds whipping up gigantic waves, and dangerous icebergs, these oceans are a sailor's nightmare. Each winter, as Earth tilts on its axis, the pole farthest from the Sun is plunged into 24-hour darkness. As the cold becomes more intense, floating layers of ice form. Joining together, they become ice floes that, bit by bit, cover the surface of the ocean. Despite their extremely harsh environments, these frozen waters are full of aquatic life, and even humans occasionally dare to venture here!

The Arctic Ocean
Situated at the northernmost tip of our planet, the Arctic Ocean is the smallest and shallowest of the oceans. It is surrounded by North America, Europe, and Asia, and is covered by a heavy sheet of ice that never completely melts. In the summer, the ice, which is 7 to 10 ft (2 to 3 m) thick, becomes thinner and breaks up in places. As these enormous plates of partially melted ice drift apart, rivers and lakes are created between them.

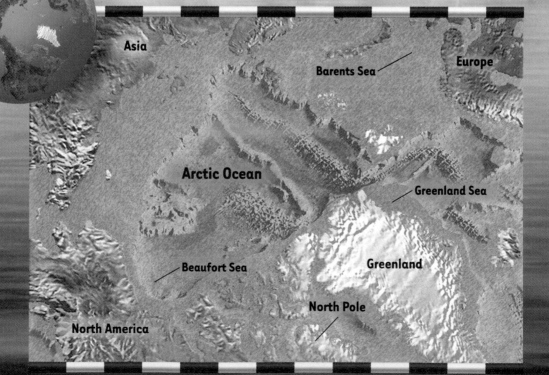

Asia

Barents Sea

Europe

Arctic Ocean

Greenland Sea

Beaufort Sea

Greenland

North Pole

North America

The Southern Ocean

Located at the southernmost end of Earth, the Southern Ocean surrounds Antarctica like a gigantic ring. Sometimes called the Antarctic Ocean, its currents flow around the continent in enormous spirals, pushing large amounts of cold water into the other oceans. These raging currents help cool our planet's tropical waters and play an important role in keeping Earth's climate in balance. The Southern Ocean is also famous for its terrifying winds, which can reach speeds of more than 185 miles per hour (300 km/h).

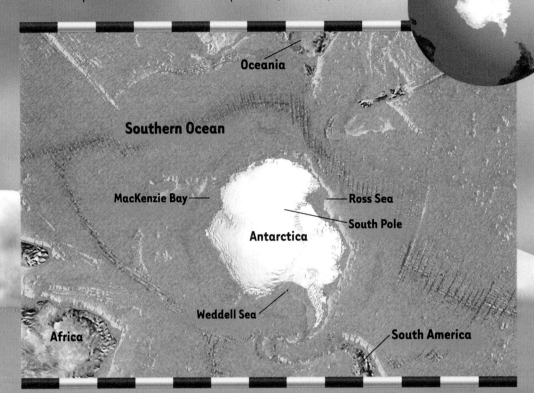

Oceania

Southern Ocean

MacKenzie Bay — — Ross Sea

— South Pole

Antarctica

Weddell Sea

Africa

South America

Icebergs

Icebergs are gigantic floating chunks of ice that have detached themselves from glaciers—enormous fields of ice that never melt. Every year, tens of thousands of icebergs fall into the ocean and drift away. Only a tiny portion of an iceberg sticks out of the water; the part hidden under the water's surface is seven times larger! Some of these castles of ice may float around for 10 years before breaking down under the effects of the Sun, wind, and waves.

The great Arctic explorers

Thousands of years ago, the Inuit people began exploring the Arctic on board their kayaks. In the late 1400s, European sailors searched for a passage through the Arctic that would take them from the Atlantic to the Pacific in a shorter amount of time, but their ships always became trapped by the ice. It was only in 1905 that Norwegian explorer Roald Amundsen became the first person to successfully make the journey by boat. In 1958, the *Nautilus* was the first submarine to cross the Arctic Ocean under the ice.

Ice giants!

The record for the biggest iceberg belongs to a giant that measured 183 miles (295 km) long and 23 miles (37 km) wide—about the size of Connecticut! Scientists are searching for ways to collect the water stored in Antarctica's enormous icebergs. Every year, the Southern Ocean produces enough icebergs to supply drinking water to half the people in the world!

Small pockets of ocean

Seas are areas of ocean that are partly or completely surrounded by continents. There are three kinds of seas. A body of water like the North Sea, for example, is called an arm of the ocean because of its wide opening to the Atlantic. Intercontinental seas like the Mediterranean are connected to the ocean by a narrow strait or passage. The Caspian Sea is an example of an inland sea. Lying completely inside the Eurasian continent, it has no link to the ocean. Inland seas are gigantic saltwater lakes. There are 54 seas on the planet, some of which have unique characteristics.

Hudson Bay

Bering Sea

North America

Gulf of Mexico

Caribbean Sea

South Am

Pacific Ocean

A huge flood

The Black Sea was once a small, freshwater lake. About 7,500 years ago, however, waters in the Mediterranean rose up, cutting through the land all the way to the lake, then spilling into it with a force more powerful than Niagara Falls! In a one-year period, people living on the shores saw their villages and fields get swallowed up by almost 500 ft (150 m) of water, the equivalent of a 50-story skyscraper!

Caribbean Sea

The Caribbean Sea is a paradise for treasure hunters! Many ships that left the Americas carrying gold and precious stones sank in these waters. The *Maravilla*, a Spanish ship that sank in 1655, was found by amateur divers in 1987. Hidden in its hold was a treasure estimated to be worth $6 billion.

Aral Sea

Since the late 1950s, the Aral Sea has lost 75 percent of its water. Freshwater rivers that once flowed into the Aral have been rerouted to water farmers' fields. Cities formerly on the coast are now several miles (km) away! With too high a concentration of salt left in the little water that remains, marine life is rapidly dying off.

Arctic Ocean

North Sea

Baltic Sea

Black Sea

Europe

Aral Sea

Asia

Sea of Okhotsk

Caspian Sea

Sea of Japan

Dead Sea

Yellow Sea

Mediterranean Sea

South China Sea

Africa

Arabian Sea

Red Sea

Bengal Bay

Oceania

Indian Ocean

Atlantic Ocean

Southern Ocean

South China Sea

Thousands of limestone islands rise up like towers in the South China Sea. Some islands are so steep that no vegetation can cling to them. This spectacular landscape is the result of a long process of erosion by water.

Mediterranean Sea

Surrounded by Europe, Africa, and the Middle East, the Mediterranean Sea has been the center of the world's great civilizations. Ancient Egyptian, Greek, and Roman cities can be found on its shores—and under its waters, too! In fact, more than 1,000 old cities have been swallowed up by the Mediterranean over time.

Dead Sea

The Dead Sea is the saltiest of all the seas. The enormous quantity of salt in the water prevents any form of aquatic life from existing here, which explains the sea's name. The dense water of the Dead Sea, thickened by salt, allows swimmers to float without any effort at all!

The faces of the coast

Wherever land and sea meet, different kinds of scenery are created, whether it consists of a sandy beach, towering cliffs, or a tiny lagoon. The coast is a place where land and sea have a powerful influence on each other, often creating a rich habitat for plants and animals. The coast is in a constant state of movement; at times, the sea swallows up part of the land, while at other times, it is the land that spreads out, extending into the sea.

Once they could walk to America

It is generally believed that the ancestors of the Native Americans came from Asia—on foot! The levels of the oceans 13,000 years ago were much lower than today. Back then, the Bering Strait, which separates Siberia and Alaska by a little more than 50 miles (80 km), was dry land. Animals, like caribou, would have traveled across this narrow bridge, followed by the humans who hunted them. A few thousand years later, the water level of the oceans rose again and flooded the strait, isolating America and its new inhabitants.

Louisiana is growing!

Measuring 250 miles (400 km) wide and extending 125 miles (200 km) from north to south, Louisiana's Mississippi Delta is large, and growing larger all the time! An enormous amount of mud and silt carried down this mighty river is continuously being deposited at the mouth of the river in the Gulf of Mexico. In this way, Louisiana is actually gaining land from the sea, growing by as much as 64 ft (20 m) a year in some areas!

TYPES OF COASTS

Delta

A delta is a vast plain in the shape of a triangle that develops where a river opens onto the ocean. North America's Mississippi River and Africa's Nile River have formed deltas.

Estuary

An estuary is a place where a river widens like a funnel and spills into a body of saltwater. North America's St. Lawrence River becomes an estuary as it reaches the Atlantic Ocean.

Lagoon

An estuary is a place where a river widens like a funnel and spills into a body of saltwater. North America's St. Lawrence River becomes an estuary as it reaches the Atlantic Ocean.

A lagoon is a small area of saltwater that is almost completely cut off from the sea by a thin arm of sand or a coral reef. One of the world's most famous lagoons is in Venice, Italy.

Ria

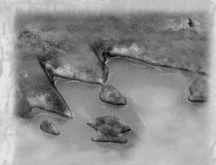

A ria, like the Ria Formosa in Portugal, is a shallow bay that cuts into a continent. It is formed when a valley is flooded by rising waters.

Fjord

A fjord is a deep and narrow U-shaped valley filled with water. Fjords are formed by the movement of glaciers. They are common to northern countries like Norway.

Cliff

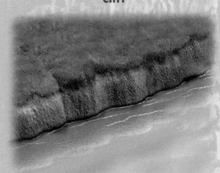

A cliff is a high wall of rock that plunges into the sea. Some of Hawaii's cliffs stand more than 3,000 feet (915 m) high!

At the bottom of the ocean

Hidden beneath the oceans of the world lies a dramatic landscape. The ocean floor features gigantic mountains, deep valleys, and vast plains. As this floor slowly moves, it gives birth to numerous volcanoes and islands, and brings traces of our planet's past back up to the surface.

Underwater landscapes

Oceans hide the most amazing underwater landscapes. Just like the continents, the ocean floor has its own plains, valleys, mountains, and canyons. The size of them can be astounding. There are undersea mountain chains that run for miles (km), trenches deep enough to swallow up Earth's tallest peaks, and vast plains that seem to stretch to infinity. Also hidden beneath the waves are thousands of volcanoes, many more than on the continents. When completely covered by water, these volcanoes are called undersea mountains. When their peaks are tall enough to break the surface of the water, they are called islands.

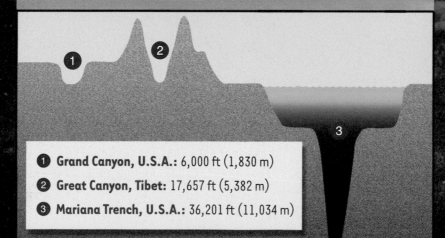

THE MARIANA TRENCH

The Mariana Trench, on the floor of the Pacific Ocean, is the deepest place on Earth. It drops as much as 36,201 ft (11,034 m) beneath the surface of the water. It is more than twice as deep as any canyon found on Earth.

1. **Grand Canyon, U.S.A.:** 6,000 ft (1,830 m)
2. **Great Canyon, Tibet:** 17,657 ft (5,382 m)
3. **Mariana Trench, U.S.A.:** 36,201 ft (11,034 m)

Continental slope
The continental slope is a steep hill at the end of the continental shelf.

Continental shelf
The continental shelf is the part of the continent that extends under the ocean in a gentle downward slope.

Abyssal plain
The abyssal plain is a vast, flat, and smooth area that begins at the foot of the continental slope.

Seamount
A seamount is a mountain that is completely submerged under water.

Submarine canyon
A submarine canyon is a narrow, deep valley found where a river spills into the ocean.

Guyot
A guyot is an underwater mountain with a flat top.

Island arc
An island arc is a group of volcanic islands.

Oceanic ridge
The oceanic ridge is a chain of underwater mountains found on either side of a long, deep crack in the seabed.

Oceanic trench
An oceanic trench is a deep, V-shaped valley that cuts into the abyssal plain.

The longest drop

The Mariana Trench is so deep that an iron ball weighing about 2 lb (1 kg) dropped from a boat would fall for about an hour before reaching the bottom.

A world in motion

Earth's crust looks like a gigantic puzzle. It is cut into about a dozen pieces, called tectonic plates. The plates float on a thick layer of magma, soft and burning-hot rock found in the center of the planet. As the magma shifts, the plates slide, meet up, and rub together. Plates crashing together may set off gigantic earthquakes. In the ocean, these events can trigger tsunamis—killer tidal waves that are dozens of feet (m) high. Over a very long period of time, the movement of plates is powerful enough to change the features of the continents and the ocean floor, carving out deep trenches and building towering chains of undersea mountains.

Mega-tsunami

In 1958, an earthquake triggered a tsunami in Alaska's Lituya Bay. It was the largest tsunami ever recorded in history. Taller than the tallest skyscrapers, this 1,720-foot (524-m) wave swallowed up the coast and destroyed millions of trees. Against all odds, a few fishers anchored in the bay survived the assault.

VOLCANIC MOUNTAINS

The movement of plates causes magma to escape from deep inside Earth. The magma cools and hardens when it comes into contact with the water or air. As it collects and builds up, the magma forms different kinds of volcanic mountains.

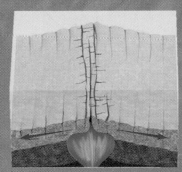

Volcanic chain
When two plates collide at the edge of a continent, the pressure becomes so great that magma starts to escape, forming a chain of volcanic mountains over time.

Oceanic ridge
When two plates move apart under the ocean, a long crack appears between them. Escaping magma builds up on both sides of the crack and forms an oceanic ridge.

Island arc
When two plates collide under the ocean, the pressure causes magma to escape. The magma forms volcanoes that grow up to the surface and become island arcs.

Continental drift
About 250 million years ago, Earth had only one continent, Pangaea, and only one ocean covered the rest of the planet. Movement in Earth's plates caused Pangaea to break up, and the separate pieces, or continents, began to drift apart. They're still moving today: the Atlantic Ocean is slowly widening, and Europe is drifting away from America, moving 1 in. (2.5 cm) farther each year.

The ocean: birthplace of islands

Thousands of islands are scattered over the world's oceans. While some are in the process of being born, others are slowly disappearing under the ocean's surface. There are several phenomena responsible for forming islands. Coral or debris may build up on the ocean floor. Rising water may completely surround a portion of land. Dropping water levels may make a shallow area appear above the surface. Most oceanic islands, however, are nothing more than the peaks of volcanic mountains rising above the water's surface. Over time, the volcano dies out, and the island, worn down by the water, disappears and becomes an undersea mountain.

HOT SPOTS: GROWING NEW VOLCANOES

Volcanoes may suddenly rise up from the middle of tectonic plates. These are called hot-spot volcanoes. A number of volcanic islands, like Hawaii, are born out of a hot spot.

active volcano
plate movement
hot spot

1. Inside Earth, a pocket of magma, called a hot spot, pierces the tectonic plate. The magma builds up to the ocean's surface, where it forms a new volcanic island.

extinct volcano

2. The plate moves, but the hot spot remains in place. Magma continues to flow upward, creating new islands.

undersea mountain

3. Volcanoes whose magma stops flowing are, over time, worn down by the ocean and become undersea mountains.

The Ring of Fire

Volcanoes usually appear along tectonic plates, where they form a sort of garland or chain. One of the best known chains is the Ring of Fire. Encircling the Pacific Ocean, it groups together most of the world's volcanoes, and includes the Aleutian Islands, Japan, and the Philippines.

From one day to the next!

In 1963, Icelanders witnessed the birth of the little island of Surtsey, about 25 miles (40 km) south of their country. An explosion was heard, and an island suddenly appeared out of the smoke! Soon after, wind and birds carried seeds to the island. Today, 45 kinds of plants and 7 species of birds make Surtsey their home!

The ocean's memory

The ocean is constantly collecting debris of all kinds. These particles drift to the bottom like snowflakes and form sediment. Over time, the sediment piles up on the ocean floor and becomes a layer of mud that may be 1,000 to 1,600 feet (300 to 500 m) thick. Some sediment comes from the remains of marine plants and animals. Some comes from land, where wind, ice, and water break down rocks into tiny pieces. These pieces are carried to the ocean by rivers, and then deposited on the seabed. Over millions of years, the sediment piles up, hardens, and is transformed into sedimentary rock. This kind of rock contains fossils, the imprints or remains of plants or animals that have been buried in the sediment. By studying fossils, we can reconstruct what life on Earth was like long ago.

One frightening fossil!

More than 350 million years ago, fishes were the masters of our planet. The largest fish, *Dunkleosteus*, was more than 16 ft (5 m) long! A number of fossils showing parts of its enormous skull and knifelike jaws have been found in the Midwest. This fierce predator devoured everything in its path, including sharks!

Fossils worth a fortune

Sometimes, many fossils are buried together in one spot, forming a kind of pocket in the sediment. Crushed by Earth's weight and cooked by its heat, this pocket of fossils is gradually turned into coal, oil, or natural gas. It is a fascinating transformation. What began as bits of dead plants and animals becomes a substance worth billions of dollars in the world market today!

FOSSILS: BITS OF TIME PRESERVED

Fossils trapped in sedimentary rock are extremely important to paleontologists, who study how life developed on Earth. Like a journey back in time, their discoveries help us understand plants and animals that no longer exist. Each layer in the sedimentary rock hides fossils belonging to a particular time period. The most recent fossils are usually found in the upper layers, and the most ancient in the lower layers. The following illustration shows how a fossil is formed.

 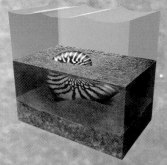  

1. An animal dies, and its body falls to the bottom of the sea.

2. Its body decomposes, but hard parts like the shell or bones are preserved and covered in sediment.

3. Over time, the sediment hardens into a rock, trapping the shell inside it and creating a fossil.

4. After millions of years, the movement of Earth's crust may expose the fossil at or near the surface.

The ocean's changing features

The ocean is an enormous mass of saltwater that is always on the move. Rocked by the winds and lifted by the tides, these waters change their temperature, salinity, and color depending on season and location. The ocean's pounding waves have the power to carve into rock and sculpt the landscape that surrounds it.

It rained an ocean

When Earth came into being 4.6 billion years ago, it had no ocean and no solid land. The planet was completely covered in a layer of boiling lava several hundred miles (km) thick. Slowly, the climate cooled, and the lava hardened to form Earth's crust. While this was taking place, volcanoes were spitting enormous amounts of water vapor into the atmosphere. As it came into contact with cold air, the water vapor stored in the atmosphere was transformed into giant clouds. Rain fell day and night for thousands of years. This flood created the first ocean, about 3.8 billion years ago.

A prehistoric bath

Water travels and is transformed, but is never lost. Since Earth was created, it has held the same amount of water, either in the form of vapor, liquid, or ice. This means that our bathtubs hold prehistoric water, the same water once bathed in by dinosaurs!

WATER'S LONG JOURNEY

The water in oceans is constantly on the move. Under the heat of the Sun, water on the surface is transformed into water vapor. The water vapor rises in the atmosphere, where it meets up with cold air and is turned into tiny droplets that form clouds. Most of the water contained in clouds falls back into the ocean in the form of rain. When it falls on the continents, rainwater travels by lakes, rivers, and underground streams to find its way back to the ocean. And the long journey starts all over again.

Heat of the sun

Wind

Cloud

Water Vapor

Lake

Ocean

Rain

River

Underground stream

The birth of an ocean

Oceans are formed when two tectonic plates move apart in the middle of a continent, creating a gigantic ditch called a continental rift. After millions of years, water from a neighboring ocean pours into this deep rift, giving birth to another ocean. This new ocean continues to grow as long as the plates continue to move apart. The Atlantic Ocean was created in this way 150 million years ago. Fifty million years from now, the East African Great Rift Valley will enlarge and fill up with water. This will break the continent and create a new sea.

The ocean's appearance

The ocean fills all our senses. We can hear its waves, smell its salty odor, and see its rippling blue surface stretching toward the horizon. Dipping our toes in it makes us shiver, and tasting it makes us wince! The ocean is an enormous soup made up of about 60 different chemical elements that give it its salty taste. The main ingredients—chlorine, sodium, sulfate, magnesium, calcium, and potassium—come mostly from river sediment dumped into the ocean. The world's saltiest waters are in the Tropics. In these regions, high temperatures and a lack of rain increase evaporation. This reduces the amount of freshwater in the ocean and raises its concentration of salt. Besides its saltiness, the ocean has several other traits, which include color, pressure, and temperature.

Water temperature
The temperature of the water depends on the intensity of the Sun's rays hitting it. It is freezing at the poles, about 30° to 40°F (-1° to 4°C), and hot in the Tropics, about 86°F (30°C). It is warmer on the surface than at a great depth, where the Sun's rays cannot penetrate and temperatures lie between 32°F (0°C) and 35°F (2°C). Seasonal changes in air temperature can also affect the temperature of the surface water by a few degrees.

Tons of salt
It would take three giant truckloads of salt to make the water in an Olympic-size swimming pool as salty as the ocean. In fact, the ocean contains so much salt that if we could extract it all, there would be enough to cover all the continents in a layer about 150 ft (45 m) deep— as high as a 15-story building!

The color of water

The colors that make up sunlight are absorbed in different ways by water particles. In ocean waters, red, yellow, and orange cannot penetrate more than a few feet (m) below the surface. Blue can penetrate more than 800 ft (245 m), making it the main color we see reflected by the ocean.

When water looks green, like in coastal waters, it is because it contains many tiny floating plants called phytoplankton. The Red Sea gets its name from the red algae that occasionally appear on its surface. The Black Sea and the Yellow Sea owe their names to the colors of the sediment floating in their waters and lying on their beds.

Caribbean Sea

The weight of water

Water puts pressure on the human body. The deeper we go, the greater the pressure. Our eardrums, which are used to the pressure of the air around us, have trouble adapting to the change. This is why our ears often hurt when we dive into water. In fact, if water pressure is too high, it can actually burst an eardrum!

Sound in water

Sound travels much better in water than in air. Marine mammals like whales use this to their advantage. Blue whales can communicate with one another even when they are separated by hundreds of miles (km)—a record-breaking distance!

Ups and downs

The wind blows on the ocean and puts its surface in motion—a steady up-and-down movement in the water called waves. If the wind blows harder, more water is moved, and the waves become larger. As popular as they may be with surfers and swimmers, waves can sometimes become a threat. A steady wind blowing at a speed of just 17 miles per hour (27 km/h) can whip up 6-foot (2-m) waves that are a danger to boats. In the middle of the ocean, sailors often face walls of water that are even higher. With the wind blowing for two days at 70 miles per hour (113 km/h), waves may be nearly 50 feet (15 m) high—as tall as a five-story building!

THE LIFE OF WAVES

Even if waves travel over long distances, the water particles in the waves do not. They only rise and fall in a circular motion created by the wind. The height of waves depends on the wind's force, the length of time the wind blows, and the distance the wind travels without being blocked by obstacles. As waves approach a coastline, they slow down and become taller and steeper. When they hit the shore, they pitch forward. These are called breaking waves.

Wind direction

The tallest waves

The shores of the island of Oahu in Hawaii see enormous waves that are often more than 30 ft (9 m) high. The tallest wave ever reported was spotted in the middle of the Pacific Ocean in 1933. It measured an incredible 112 ft (34 m) in height!

Crest
The crest is the top of the wave.

Height
The height of the wave is the distance between the wave's crest and its trough.

Trough
The trough is the lowest part of the wave.

Breaking wave
Breaking waves are the waves that collapse into foam on the coasts.

World travelers

Large currents of water flow through the world's oceans, taking precise routes. Currents that circulate on the water's surface are pushed by Earth's prevailing winds and can travel more than 30 miles (50 km) a day. If the currents begin in tropical zones, their waters are warm; if they start off near the poles, they are cold. Deep currents are formed under polar ice floes, which are large sheets of floating ice. In these regions, cold, heavy saltwater sinks and pushes the water that lies underneath it toward the equator. The direction that currents take is affected by the shorelines of continents and by Earth's rotation. In the Northern Hemisphere, currents flow clockwise; in the Southern Hemisphere, they move in the opposite direction. As currents stir up the planet's waters, they supply heat, oxygen, and food to all the oceans. Currents are also important to a number of marine species. Young eels benefit from currents like the Gulf Stream. They use it like a superhighway to take them from the Tropics all the way to North America or Europe.

Nice to be warm

The water of the Gulf Stream current is sometimes 18°F (10°C) warmer than the ocean around it. Hot enough to affect the climate in northern countries, the Gulf Stream brings tropical fish all the way up to Cape Cod, Massachusetts, and helps palm trees grow in Ireland!

THE GULF STREAM

The Gulf Stream is a warm-water current that starts in the Gulf of Mexico, runs along the coast of the United States, and then heads northeast across the Atlantic Ocean to Europe.

Warm-water current

Europe

North America

Atlantic Ocean

Africa

See map page 91

The El Niño current

Near Peru, trade winds usually push warm water westward, away from Peru's shores. When this happens, cold water rises up from the bottom of the ocean to take the place of the warm water. These cold waters are full of food, attracting large numbers of fishes that come to feed.

Every four to seven years, however, the trade winds weaken and a warm current, called El Niño, forms near the coast. El Niño is Spanish for "the Christ Child." The nickname was given to the current because it usually appears around Christmastime. El Niño is responsible for the deaths of many sea creatures and greatly harms the fishing industry. By throwing the climate off balance, disastrous effects may be felt all over the planet. El Niño causes extremely heavy rainfall in South America and the United States, violent hurricanes in the Pacific, and a serious shortage of rain in Australia and Asia.

PREVAILING WINDS

Great winds travel the surface of our planet. They always blow with the same force and move in the same direction. Called prevailing winds, they are the result of large currents of warm and cool air mixing together. There are three types of prevailing wind: west winds, trade winds, and polar winds.

Polar winds
Polar winds are cold, powerful, and violent. Near the Antarctic, these winds are so fierce that sailors have nicknamed the latitude where they blow the "Screaming Sixties."

Trade winds
Trade winds are strong and steady. They helped the great explorers of the past sail across the Atlantic Ocean to discover the New World.

West winds
West winds are very strong, particularly in the Southern Hemisphere, where they create gigantic waves. Navigation here is so dangerous that sailors have nicknamed these latitudes the "Roaring Forties" and the "Furious Fifties."

Doldrums
The doldrums is the name given to a calm, almost windless zone located near the equator. This region was long dreaded by sailors, whose sailboats could become trapped for weeks at a time, waiting for a breeze to carry them out.

Polar winds

The influence of space

Twice a day, the ocean rises up to cover the shore, and then sinks back. This regular phenomenon, called the tide, is set in motion by astral bodies! The Moon, the Sun, and Earth attract one another, as do all astral bodies in the universe. Because the Moon is closest to Earth, it has the strongest influence over the tides. Like a giant magnet, the Moon pulls the ocean toward itself, making it bulge upward. The shape of the coastline and the depth of the water affect the heights of tides. In shallow inland seas, tides are almost impossible to detect. In bays open to the ocean, however, they can be quite spectacular!

Record tides

At the head of the Bay of Fundy in Canada, the tide sometimes reaches 52 ft (16 m)—as high as a five-story building! A record tide is produced there because the ocean water is pushed into the funnel-shaped bay. On the other side of the Atlantic Ocean, at Mont St. Michel in France, the tide covers an extremely wide area. At low tide, the ocean moves back about 6 miles (10 km)!

HOW TIDES ARE FORMED

Where a large body of water faces the Moon, the Moon's attractive force pulls the water upward, causing a high tide in that part of the world. Earth's rotation causes an identical high tide on the opposite side of the globe. In between these two high-tide zones, low tides occur. In this way, the ocean is always rising in two places in the world and lowering in two other areas. The tides may be large (spring tides) or small (neap tides), depending on the way Earth, the Moon, and the Sun are lined up during the month.

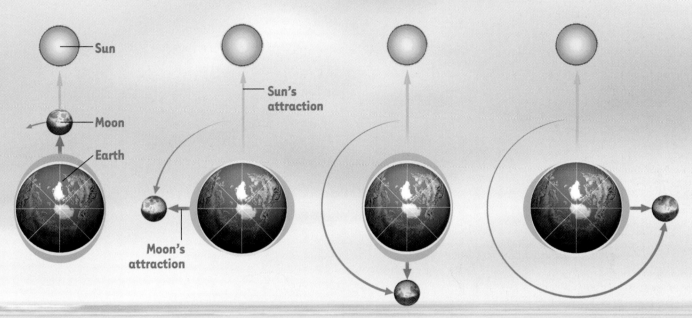

Spring tide

During the new-moon phase, the Sun and the Moon form a straight line with Earth. Their attracting forces unite to make the ocean rise to its fullest, producing a large tide.

Neap tide

When the Moon is in the first-quarter phase, its attracting force is partly canceled out by the Sun's attracting force. This produces a small tide.

Spring tide

During the full-moon phase, the Sun and the Moon are again in line with Earth. As Earth's rotation causes an identical high tide to occur on two opposite sides of the planet, the astral bodies join forces once more to produce a large tide.

Neap tide

When the Moon is in the last-quarter phase, its attracting force is again canceled out by the Sun, producing a small tide.

Sculpting the coastline

Waves, currents, tides, and storms attack the coast, breaking off pieces of land and depositing them somewhere else. This natural phenomenon is called erosion. The ocean is endlessly moving the sand on the shore, making a beach smaller in one area and enlarging it in another. On rocky coasts, the water erodes the softer parts of cliffs, forming cracks, digging caves, and carving majestic sculptures. Whether made of sand or rock, the appearance of coastal landscapes is constantly changed by water.

FROM A CLIFF TO A REEF

When a cliff extends outward into the ocean in a point, it forms a cape. The cape is easily eroded because it is battered by waves on every side. This is how a cliff can turn into a reef.

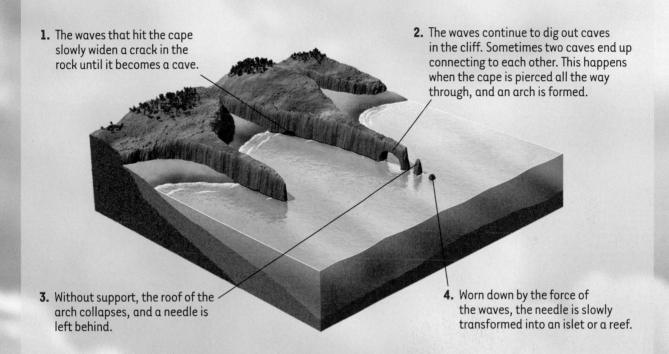

1. The waves that hit the cape slowly widen a crack in the rock until it becomes a cave.

2. The waves continue to dig out caves in the cliff. Sometimes two caves end up connecting to each other. This happens when the cape is pierced all the way through, and an arch is formed.

3. Without support, the roof of the arch collapses, and a needle is left behind.

4. Worn down by the force of the waves, the needle is slowly transformed into an islet or a reef.

Sandy beach

Erosion is responsible for creating beaches. The billions of grains of sand on a beach are often made of tiny bits of rock that have been carried away by rivers and ocean currents, and then pushed up on the shore. The sand may also come from the skeletons of sea creatures that the ocean has reduced to crumbs.

Beaches of amazing colors!

Some beaches are as white as snow, while others are as black as night. The color of the sand depends on where it comes from. The black sand of volcanic islands is a mix of ashes and bits of hardened lava. The white sand of tropical beaches comes from animals. It is often made up of splintered seashells, coral fragments, and even tropical fish excrement!

An ocean of life

From the Tropics to the poles, and from its surface to its deepest trenches, the ocean is home to an amazing variety of strange and unique creatures. Many of these have remained unknown until quite recently. Only a small fraction of the ocean bottom has been thoroughly explored by humans. Who knows what lies hidden in the 116 million square miles (300 million sq km) still to be discovered?

An ocean full of life

Life appeared in the ocean about 3.8 billion years ago. Its first inhabitants were neither animals nor plants, but microscopic creatures called bacteria. Over time, some bacteria used the Sun's energy to make oxygen, the gas that allows plants and animals to survive. Once there was oxygen, life in the ocean was changed forever. Sponges, jellyfish, worms, and starfish appeared in turn. Fishes followed millions of years later. Some of these fishes' descendants developed lungs and legs. They learned to breathe and to move around on land. They grew into amphibians such as frogs. They were followed by reptiles, birds, and mammals. Even though a large number of animals today live on the land, the ocean is still home to most creatures. In fact, 80 percent of the animals on Earth live in the water! The principal marine groups are sponges, cnidarians, worms, mollusks, echinoderms, crustaceans, fishes, reptiles, and mammals.

Marine reptiles
Like fishes, marine reptiles are covered in scales. However, they do not have gills to filter oxygen and must breathe outside the water. Marine reptiles include eight species of sea turtles, a few kinds of sea snakes, and one species of sea lizard.

Cnidarians
The cnidarian group includes jellyfish, anemones, and corals. These marine animals have tentacles that can inject paralyzing venom into their prey.

Crustaceans
Crabs, shrimp, lobsters, and other crustaceans are cousins to land insects. Their bodies are protected by a hard shell. Crustaceans are equipped with antennas to help them to detect movement as well as jointed legs. Some crustaceans have pincers, or claws, which they use to defend themselves.

Echinoderms
Echinoderms include animals with spiny skins, like starfish and urchins. Their bodies are composed of five identical parts that branch out like the spokes on a wheel.

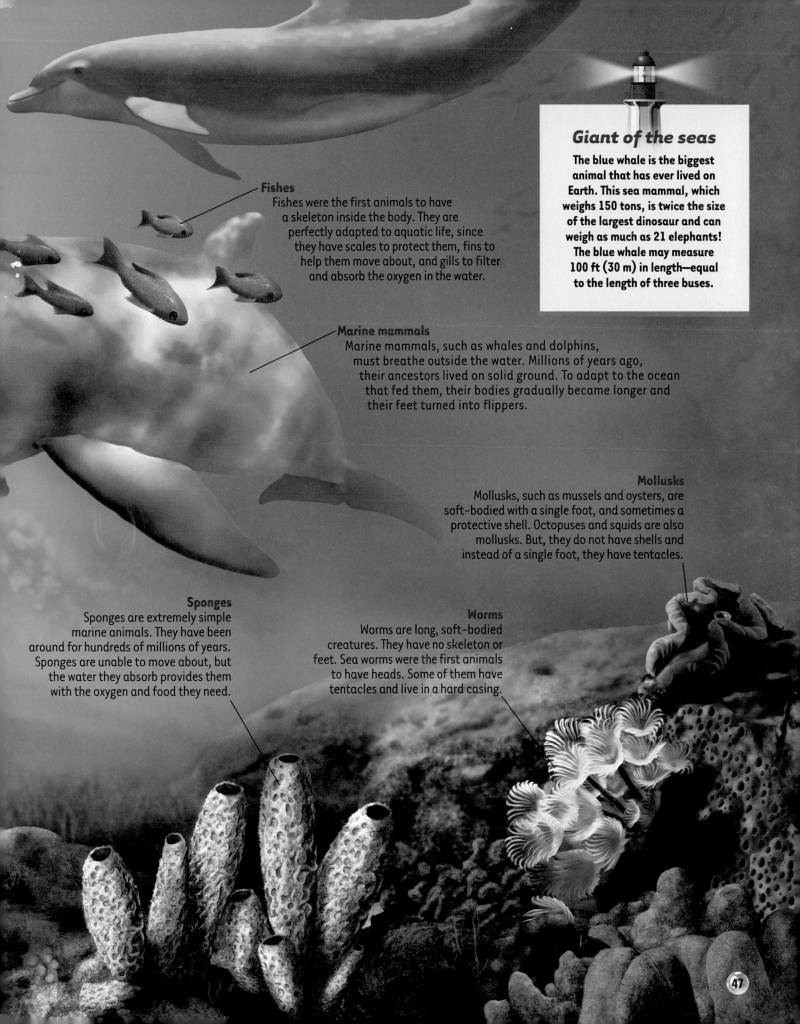

Fishes
Fishes were the first animals to have a skeleton inside the body. They are perfectly adapted to aquatic life, since they have scales to protect them, fins to help them move about, and gills to filter and absorb the oxygen in the water.

Giant of the seas
The blue whale is the biggest animal that has ever lived on Earth. This sea mammal, which weighs 150 tons, is twice the size of the largest dinosaur and can weigh as much as 21 elephants! The blue whale may measure 100 ft (30 m) in length—equal to the length of three buses.

Marine mammals
Marine mammals, such as whales and dolphins, must breathe outside the water. Millions of years ago, their ancestors lived on solid ground. To adapt to the ocean that fed them, their bodies gradually became longer and their feet turned into flippers.

Mollusks
Mollusks, such as mussels and oysters, are soft-bodied with a single foot, and sometimes a protective shell. Octopuses and squids are also mollusks. But, they do not have shells and instead of a single foot, they have tentacles.

Sponges
Sponges are extremely simple marine animals. They have been around for hundreds of millions of years. Sponges are unable to move about, but the water they absorb provides them with the oxygen and food they need.

Worms
Worms are long, soft-bodied creatures. They have no skeleton or feet. Sea worms were the first animals to have heads. Some of them have tentacles and live in a hard casing.

Who eats what?

A herring is slowly digesting its meal of shrimp when it is suddenly swallowed up by a porpoise, which is then devoured by a killer whale! This process, in which one species is eaten by the next in line, is called the food chain. The ocean's food chain starts with tiny floating algae called phytoplankton. Phytoplankton feed plant-eating marine animals called herbivores. Herbivores are eaten by meat-eaters called carnivores. No matter where they are in the food chain, every plant or animal in the ocean is part of a complex and fragile network in which each species depends on other species for survival.

A crowd of krill

Krill are small crustaceans about 2 to 3 in. (5 to 7 cm) long that look like shrimp. In the cold waters of the Southern Ocean, krill live in gigantic groups that resemble carpets spread out over the ocean's surface. There are 600,000 billion of these creatures in the world, making them the most plentiful animal on the planet. This is a good thing for the blue whale, which can eat as many as 40 million krill in a single day!

THE FOOD CHAIN

Phytoplankton use the Sun's energy as well as nutrients dissolved in the water to produce oxygen and to grow. Phytoplankton are eaten by tiny, floating marine animals called zooplankton. Zooplankton, in turn, feed small fishes. The small fishes are eaten by bigger fishes, which are then devoured by large predators, like the killer whale. At the bottom of the ocean are decomposers. They feed on bits of dead animals and plants that have drifted down from the surface. Decomposers absorb the leftovers and turn them into nourishing substances. The currents bring these substances back to the surface, where they are used by phytoplankton, making the chain complete.

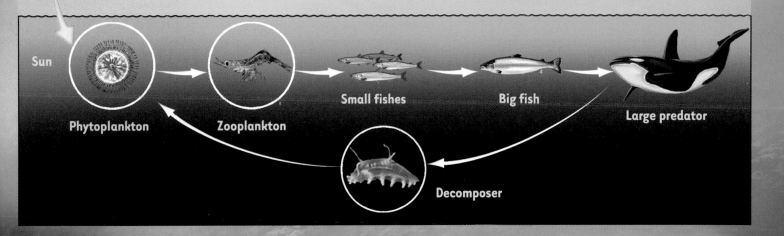

Sun

Phytoplankton

Zooplankton

Small fishes

Big fish

Large predator

Decomposer

Blue whale in a group of krill

Armed and ready

Marine animals have ways of escaping and hunting that sometimes seem amusing and sometimes are quite terrifying. While one creature's tactic is to use its shell as a shield, another animal's trick is to disguise itself to look like its surroundings. The box jellyfish has a powerful weapon—poisonous venom that can kill a human in just four minutes! If a predator catches a starfish by one of its arms, the starfish can escape by leaving the arm behind. It grows back later. For safety, several small fish may swim close together in a school, pretending they are one large fish.

This kind of cooperation exists among predators, too. Killer whales and dolphins hunt in packs so they can surround their prey. Although a trick may be very effective, it doesn't work all of the time.

Secondhand shell
Unlike other crabs, the hermit crab has no shell. To protect itself, it borrows an empty shell left by a mollusk and hides underneath it. As the hermit crab grows larger, it has to look for a bigger home.

Ace hunter

With its powerful jaws and pointed teeth as sharp as knives, the great white shark is one of the ocean's most dangerous predators. It is also the largest of the carnivorous fishes. Using its never-failing sense of smell, the great white can locate prey miles (km) away. It could even find a single drop of blood in an Olympic-size pool!

Poison stone
The stonefish is the deadliest poisonous fish. It hides on the sea bottom, disguising itself as a stone and covering itself in algae. Remaining completely still, it can kill whatever touches the venomous spines of its dorsal fin.

Streams of ink
When an octopus is chased or senses danger nearby, it shoots out a jet of ink, which clouds up the surrounding water. Hidden from its predator, the octopus uses the opportunity to make its escape.

Heads or tails?
The threadfin butterfly fish is marked by a spot near its tail that looks like an eye. The fish's real eyes in front are disguised. Predators become completely confused by this fish that appears to be escaping backward!

A dish that bites back
When it senses danger is near, the porcupine fish fills its stomach with water and expands like a balloon. Its prickly spines, which usually lie flat against its body, stand on end. Predators rapidly lose their urge to take a bite.

Comforting arms
The small clown fish finds comfort among the poisonous tentacles of sea anemones. The fish's body is coated with a sticky substance that protects it from the anemones' venom. No predator dares to go after the clown fish in its shelter.

Funny nose
The sawfish has a nose that measures about 6 ft (2 m) in length. Its nose is an effective tool. It can dig around in the muddy seabed to search for prey, and can be used like a stick to hit and stun fish swimming together in a group.

Under the sunlight

The sunlit zone is the first of three zones in the ocean. It is the layer of water that extends from the surface to a depth of 650 feet (200 m). At this level, the Sun's rays easily pass through the water, bringing light and comfortable temperatures. It encourages the growth of plants, which in turn attract many animals. This means that life is most plentiful and varied close to the surface. The sunlit zone is like a hunting ground, and the animals living here rely on speed and excellent vision for survival. Predators have bodies that are tapered, like torpedoes, to let them cut through the water quickly. Their prey, on the other hand, have many tricks for escaping their predators' sharp eyes.

A big appetite
A bluefin tuna may be 10 ft (3 m) long and weigh more than 1,100 lbs (500 kg). This gigantic fish has a streamlined body built for fast swimming in the high seas. It uses so much energy swimming that it must eat the equivalent of a quarter of its weight in food every day.

Sunlit zone
650 ft (200 m)

Twilight zone
3,300 ft (1,000 m)

Midnight zone

A speed champion
The swordfish beats all speed records for swimming by moving at 68 mph (110 km/h). This fast fish is 13 ft (4 m) long and is perfectly designed for speed. It cuts through water near the surface like a jet plane through the skies.

Surface disguises

It is difficult to pass unnoticed in the clear waters of the sunlit zone. This is why many prey, such as zooplankton, are tiny and transparent. Some fishes that live near the surface have dark backs and pale bellies. Seen from above, they disappear into the gloom of the water below them. Looked at from below, they blend in with the light at the surface. Other fishes are completely silver-colored. Their skin reflects the sunlight like mirrors, making it difficult for their prey to see them.

A fish that flies

To escape its predators, the flying fish makes a dash to the surface and leaps out of the water. By lifting its long fins and hitting the waves with its tail, the flying fish can glide over the water almost 600 ft (180 m).

Sailing on the waves

The Portuguese man-of-war is equipped with a pneumatophore, an organ that resembles a large float. This allows it to drift on the surface, sailing with the currents. The man-of-war's venomous tentacles, which can measure more than 65 ft (20 m) in length, catch and paralyze prey as it moves along.

Swim or sink

There are more blue sharks found around the world than any other kind of shark. Like all sharks, the blue shark lacks a swim bladder, the organ that allows a fish to float. To remain near the surface without sinking, this 13-foot-long (4-m) predator must swim nonstop day and night.

An excellent swimmer

The leatherback turtle is the largest of the sea turtles. This endangered species measures almost 7 ft (2 m) long and weighs over 1,100 lbs (500 kg). The leatherback is the only turtle without scales. Its smooth shell and its oar-shaped legs help this giant swim more than 325 ft (100 m) in just 10 seconds.

The high seas

Rivers dump a variety of food into coastal waters. This encourages the growth of plants and attracts marine animals. As a result, there is more life to be found near the coast and far less as one heads into high seas. Some animals, however, manage to survive this far from shore, even though their prey is scattered over a wide area. Certain species of sharks and whales are used to traveling long distances at high speeds in their hunt for food.

Keeping an eye open

Dolphins must regularly return to the surface of the water to breathe. Since a simple nap could cause them to drown, they can never fall entirely asleep. Dolphins deal with this by allowing only one-half of their brains to go to sleep at a time. The other half remains awake so the dolphin can go up for air and also watch out for predators.

An unfriendly neighborhood

The twilight zone is a layer of ocean between the clear waters near the surface and the blackness of the midnight zone beneath it. At this depth, 650 to 3,300 feet (200 to 1,000 m) below the surface, the Sun's rays barely pierce the darkness. Without sunlight, no plants can survive, and food is scarce. The creatures living here often wait for scraps, waste matter, and bodies of dead animals to sink from above. You would think that few animals could survive in such an unfriendly neighborhood. Yet the twilight zone is home to thousands of species who have developed unique ways to cope with difficult living conditions.

In search of a nighttime snack
Like several other animals, the lantern fish leaves the twilight zone at night. Under cover of darkness, it travels to the surface, where there is more nutritious food to be found.

Sunlit zone
650 ft (200 m)

Twilight zone
3,300 ft (1,000 m)

Midnight zone

Using its head
The deep-sea anglerfish, which lives about 1,000 to 13,000 ft (300 to 4,000 m) below the surface, has its own "fishing rod." This baiting device, containing bioluminescent bacteria, dangles from the fish's head—and leads prey to its large, waiting mouth.

Bioluminescence

In the darkness of the twilight zone, 9 out of 10 living organisms can use natural chemicals to produce their own light. This is called bioluminescence. Animals may use their light to attract prey, to scare off predators, to identify one another, and to communicate.

No meal is too big

With its mouthful of long, curved teeth that work like skewers, the viper fish is very skilled at catching prey. The stomach of the viper fish can expand and its jaws can open wide enough to swallow and digest prey almost as big as itself!

A trick of the light

With points of light dotting its belly, the hatchet fish enjoys a handy disguise. Predators swimming below have trouble spotting the hatchet fish because they confuse its glow with the Sun's rays filtering through the water.

See-through sea creatures

Several animals of the twilight zone have transparent bodies, like that of the vitreledonella octopus. Jellylike, colorless, and transparent, this octopus has an easy time escaping the view of its predators.

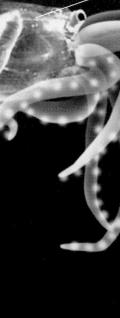

Teamwork

Siphonophores are animals that light up and live attached to one another. Each of them has a job to do. While some capture prey, others digest food, reproduce, or help the colony move about. A giant siphonophore group can be 131 ft (40 m) long—longer than the world's biggest single animal, the blue whale.

Pioneers of the deep

In 1934, scientists William Beebe and Otis Barton went where no one had ever gone before, descending 3,028 ft (923 m) beneath the ocean's surface. Their record-breaking adventure was made possible thanks to one of their own inventions: the bathysphere, a steel bubble measuring about 5 ft (1.5 m) in diameter. While sitting inside the bathysphere, which was attached to a ship by a steel cable, the two men were able to observe underwater animals that had never been seen by humans.

Together forever

The deep-sea anglerfish can't live without his mate! This tiny fish, about the size of your little finger, spends his whole life attached to the body of his female partner. With his teeth sunk into her skin, he sucks her blood to get the nutrients he needs to survive—a practical way to deal with a food shortage!

The creatures of the darkest depths

The midnight zone lies more than 3,300 feet (1,000 m) beneath the surface. Here, the darkness is complete, the pressure is crushing, the cold is intense, and food is scarce. In adapting to this hostile environment, the creatures that live in this zone have developed rather nightmarish appearances. Their bodies are soft and jellylike to help them withstand the pressure. Their mouths are gigantic, which increases their chances of gulping down any rare prey that may be passing by. Bioluminescent creatures can still be found higher up in the midnight zone. The deeper one goes, however, the less bioluminescence occurs. As the sense of sight becomes useless, creatures living in the deepest part of the ocean are either blind or have no eyes. Sensitive to the tiniest vibrations, however, they wait patiently for prey to brush against them in the dark, or for food to sink down from the surface.

Precious sponge
The glass sponge, which resembles a magnificent crystal palace, lives attached to the sea bottom. Its delicate skeleton is made of many tiny pieces that look like snowflakes.

Sunlit zone
650 ft (200 m)

Twilight zone
3,300 ft (1,000 m)

Midnight zone

Giant tadpole
The rat-tail is the most plentiful fish living at a great depth. These creatures can be found on the bottom of every ocean in the world. Measuring about 3 ft (1 m) in length, with a large head and a long tail, the rat-tail resembles a giant tadpole.

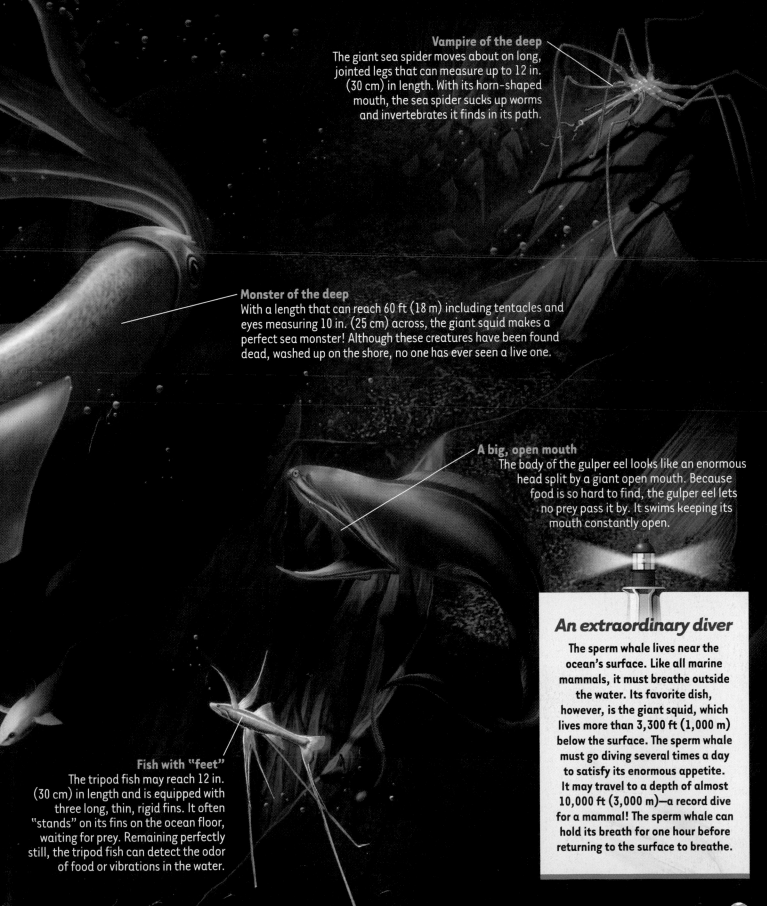

Vampire of the deep
The giant sea spider moves about on long, jointed legs that can measure up to 12 in. (30 cm) in length. With its horn-shaped mouth, the sea spider sucks up worms and invertebrates it finds in its path.

Monster of the deep
With a length that can reach 60 ft (18 m) including tentacles and eyes measuring 10 in. (25 cm) across, the giant squid makes a perfect sea monster! Although these creatures have been found dead, washed up on the shore, no one has ever seen a live one.

A big, open mouth
The body of the gulper eel looks like an enormous head split by a giant open mouth. Because food is so hard to find, the gulper eel lets no prey pass it by. It swims keeping its mouth constantly open.

Fish with "feet"
The tripod fish may reach 12 in. (30 cm) in length and is equipped with three long, thin, rigid fins. It often "stands" on its fins on the ocean floor, waiting for prey. Remaining perfectly still, the tripod fish can detect the odor of food or vibrations in the water.

An extraordinary diver
The sperm whale lives near the ocean's surface. Like all marine mammals, it must breathe outside the water. Its favorite dish, however, is the giant squid, which lives more than 3,300 ft (1,000 m) below the surface. The sperm whale must go diving several times a day to satisfy its enormous appetite. It may travel to a depth of almost 10,000 ft (3,000 m)—a record dive for a mammal! The sperm whale can hold its breath for one hour before returning to the surface to breathe.

Springs at the bottom

In a freezing cold environment more than 6,500 feet (2,000 m) deep, mysterious springs spit jets of water whose temperatures are close to 750°F (400°C). These underwater fountains, called deep-sea hydrothermal vents, are located in volcanic zones, particularly around oceanic ridges. They are formed when water breaks through cracks in the Earth's crust, heats up as it comes in contact with magma, and then shoots up out of the ground like a geyser. As the boiling hot water comes in contact with cold water, the metals and chemical elements in the hot water form clouds of ash. The ash settles on the ocean floor in a series of layers, building up over time into tall chimneys. This hostile environment where boiling and freezing water come together is full of toxic gases that leak from the vents. Surprisingly, the areas around hydrothermal vents are densely populated by a wide variety of unique creatures.

Gigantic mollusks
Giant clams gather by the hundreds around hydrothermal vents. These animals, whose shells can measure almost 12 in. (30 cm) in size, have bacteria living in their gills. The bacteria use the sulfur from the vents to produce the nourishment these mollusks need.

Predators with no mercy
White crabs, which can grow to almost 5 in. (13 cm) in length, are the most savage creatures living around hydrothermal vents. They gather around the chimneys in massive groups and eat bacteria as well as shrimp and mollusks. Sometimes they even devour each other.

Underwater towers

Hydrothermal chimneys can grow to incredible heights. The most impressive one found to date was discovered off the coast of Oregon. It measures nearly 40 ft (12 m) across and stands almost 150 ft (45 m) high—as tall as a 15-story building! This towering chimney has been nicknamed Godzilla, after the huge movie monster.

A unique ecosystem

Many bacteria live close to hydrothermal vents. These microorganisms develop and grow with the help of the toxic hydrogen sulfide that leaks out of the vents. The abundance of bacteria attracts many animals, which in turn feed a number of carnivores. In this way, the bacteria are the first link in an exceptional food chain—the only one on Earth that does not depend on the Sun!

Alvin and its extraordinary discovery

On board the submersible *Alvin* in 1977, three researchers discovered the existence of hydrothermal vents. To their great surprise, they found a gathering of strange-looking, gigantic animals 8,200 ft (2,500 m) beneath the surface. The scientists rapidly made the link between this living oasis and the burning hot springs nearby. They noted that a number of creatures had tubes, shells, or carapaces to protect them from the heat and poisonous gases. Thanks to *Alvin*'s discovery, more than 300 new species of animals were identified.

A foot in boiling water

The Pompeii worm is the animal that lives closest to the vents. This 5-inch (13-cm) worm endures extreme conditions better than any other creature. The temperature of the water near its head is about 68°F (20°C) and the temperature at its tail end, resting directly on the chimney, is close to 175°F (80°C)!

Giant worm

The tube worm, which can measure up to 10 ft (3 m) long, lives in a protective tube close to the hydrothermal vents. The tube worm lacks a mouth and a digestive system, but it harbors bacteria in its body that supply the nourishment it needs.

A fish without scales

The zoarcid, or eelpout, is one of the rare fishes living near the hydrothermal vents. Its long, flat, white body has no scales. This predator, which measures almost 2 ft (60 cm) in length, swims slowly and feeds on small invertebrates such as shrimps.

Creatures of the cold

Even though humans never dare to dip their little toes in, life is plentiful in the polar oceans, especially in spring and summer. Once the ice begins to melt, tiny algae that have been locked in the ice are set free. The sudden abundance of food attracts zooplankton and krill, which in turn attract larger animals, like migratory birds and whales. When winter returns, many of these aquatic animals prefer to migrate to warmer waters. Others, like penguins, choose to stay at the South Pole in winter, far away from large predators. Most polar animals depend on the ocean for survival. The land, which is often covered in a thick layer of ice, has almost nothing to offer.

The unicorn of the Arctic

The narwhal is a rare type of whale. There are approximately 30,000 of them in the Arctic Ocean. It measures from 13 to 16 ft (4 to 5 m) in length and does not have dorsal fins on its back, which allows it to swim directly under the ice without hurting itself. The single tooth of the male narwhal grows into the shape of a long horn. It is mainly used in battles with other males.

Wings for swimming

The emperor penguin is a seabird of the South Pole that cannot fly. It is, however, an excellent swimmer, and uses its wings like flippers to propel itself up to 37 mph (60 km/h) underwater. In winter, when temperatures may drop to as low as -76°F (-60°C), several thousand penguins huddle together to keep warm.

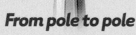

From pole to pole

The arctic tern spends almost its entire life flying! Every year, it travels a loop of about 19,000 to 25,000 miles (30,000 to 40,000 km) from the North Pole to the South Pole and back. This migration pattern gives the arctic tern a chance to enjoy the plentiful food and long sunny days at each pole at the best time of year. This little world traveler holds the long-distance record for migration in the animal kingdom.

Well padded

The walrus is an aquatic mammal of the Arctic that weighs close to a ton. A single walrus meal may consist of 4,000 clams! Its tusks, which can measure 3 ft (1 m) in length, are used in combat. They also help the walrus to heave its huge body onto the ice and to dislodge shellfish from the ocean floor.

Master diver
The Weddell seal can hunt almost 2,000 ft (600 m) deep and hold its breath for close to an hour. This mammal spends most of its time under the ice in the frigid waters of the Southern Ocean. It uses its teeth to cut holes in the ice so it can come up for air after diving.

Invisible hunter
The polar bear can measure 8.5 ft (2.6 m) in length and weigh 1,760 lbs (800 kg)—the equivalent of a small car! Its white fur makes it invisible when hunting on the ice. This huge and tireless carnivore can also swim for hours as it hunts for seals and fish.

Polar terror
The orca has pointed teeth and a powerful jaw. This unstoppable killer whale can pursue its prey onto a floating sheet of ice, either by sliding on the ice or by using its head to break through from below. It even attacks polar bears and other kinds of whales.

Antarctic icefish
Like the hundreds of other species of fishes that live in the freezing waters of the Southern Ocean, the antarctic icefish produces a natural antifreeze. Its blood contains special molecules that attach to ice crystals as they form, preventing their bodies from freezing, even at subzero temperatures.

Keeping warm
The animals of the freezing oceans have remarkable features that protect them from the cold. Seals and whales have a thick layer of fat under their skin, which insulates them and, at the same time, stores up extra energy. To shield themselves from the icy waters, certain feathered or furred animals secrete a waterproof oil. Other animals produce a kind of antifreeze that circulates in their bodies.

Living mosaics

There are about 700 different species of coral. They come in many different forms, and may look like cauliflower, fan shapes, or even pipe organs. Some are soft, while others are as hard as rock. Coral is made up of polyps, which are tiny animals that belong to the sea anemone family. Some of these soft-bodied creatures with no skeletons secrete limestone, a hard substance that acts like a protective armor. When a polyp dies, its limestone armor survives intact. The great reefs of the world consist of thousands of generations of dead polyps, piled one on top of the other. Coral reefs attract a variety of animals in search of food and a safe place to hide. Almost a third of all species of fish live in this fragile environment, which is threatened by pollution, global warming, and fishing.

Relying on each other
The beautiful colors we see in coral come from the many microscopic algae they shelter. Algae provide the oxygen and food necessary for the growth of coral. In return, the coral's waste serves as fertilizer to help the algae grow. Because algae need heat and light to live, coral grows in warm, shallow water. Coral can be found near the Tropics, mainly in the Indian and Pacific oceans.

The Great Barrier Reef
Australia's Great Barrier Reef covers a total area of about 135,000 square miles (350,000 sq km) —almost the size of Montana. It is the largest structure ever built by living creatures! It has taken millions of years to grow the Great Barrier Reef, which appeared on Earth long before humans did.

Coral killers
Crown-of-thorns starfish can overrun coral and devour it, sometimes destroying part of a reef. These hungry creatures, which can measure almost 31 in. (80 cm) across, crush the coral and feed off the soft polyps inside it.

Types of reefs

There are three types of coral reefs: fringing reefs, barrier reefs, and atolls. A fringing reef runs along a coast, while a barrier reef is separated from land by a thin stretch of water. An atoll is a ring of coral encircling a shallow body of water called a lagoon. An atoll develops when a fringing reef surrounds a volcanic island. Although the coral never stops growing, the volcanic island is slowly worn down by erosion and ends up being completely underwater. Over thousands of years, the space formerly occupied by the volcanic island is replaced by a lagoon surrounded by a ring of coral!

Quite a bite
The powerful teeth of the parrot fish help it to finely grind the coral that it eats. Once the coral is digested, it is transformed into white sand. A parrot fish excretes an enormous amount of sand—between 1 and 5 tons each year!

Night predator
The moray eel is a fierce fish that usually measures from 2 to 5 ft (0.6 to 1.5 m) in length. By day, it hides most of its long body in the rocks, allowing only its head to stick out. The moray waits for nighttime to hunt for prey.

Razor-sharp
When it senses danger, the surgeonfish changes color and suddenly raises spines as sharp as razor blades on its tail. This colorful fish cleans coral by eating the excess algae that cover it.

Cleaning service
The cleaner wrasse feeds on the parasites that collect around the mouths, fins, and gills of other fish. The services provided by the cleaner wrasse are so appreciated that the other fish actually line up for its help. The cleaner wrasse can serve up to 2,500 "clients" per day—that's almost two a minute!

Between land and sea

Animals of the coast invent many strategies for surviving the waves and tides that soak them and then dry them out. On sandy coasts, these creatures hide under the damp sand, protected from the waves, their predators, and the Sun's burning rays. On rocky coasts, algae and animals cling to the stone to avoid being washed away by the waves. If they have nothing to hide under, animals keep from drying out in the sun by ducking into cracks, tufts of damp algae, or rock pools left by the tide. Animals of any coast must also be on the lookout for predators, which hunt from the land, the sea, and even the sky!

Colorful shells
Countless periwinkles populate the rocky coasts, feeding on algae. These tiny mollusks with colorful shells live according to the rhythm of the tides. Periwinkles can drown if they remain underwater for too long.

Keeping a lookout
The cockle is a type of mollusk. Burying itself under the sand, the cockle breathes through a tube called a siphon. The siphon also works like a periscope, allowing the cockle to survey its surroundings while remaining well hidden from predators.

A watchman on the floor
The sole lives on the ocean bottom. Lying on its side, this flat fish covers its body with sand to disguise itself. Its two eyes, which are located on one side of its head, allow it to see whatever passes above it.

A picky eater
The oystercatcher is a bird that hunts the coast in search of food. When mealtime arrives, the oystercatcher uses its long, thin beak to pick into a shell, cracking it open with a hard tap to get to the mollusk inside.

In a single handful of sand

Every handful of sand hides countless living organisms. Among these grains of sand are millions of microscopic animals and algae as well as billions of bacteria. With careful observation, one can even spot dozens of tiny animals like worms and miniature crayfish.

Teamwork
Mussels live in colonies on rocky coasts. To resist the waves, they cling together and attach themselves to the rock with the help of strong threads. At low tide, mussels close their shells completely to conserve moisture and avoid drying out.

Feather duster
The serpulid worm lives inside a protective tube. At high tide, this feather duster worm puts out its tentacles to catch its prey. At low tide, it disappears into its tube, which it closes up with a flattened tentacle to keep from drying out.

Creatures with claws
At low tide, the large number of crabs that live on the coast hide under rocks and algae or in rock pools, waiting for the return of the high tide. All crabs have eight legs and two claws that can grow back if they are torn off.

Gardens in the ocean

Marine plants play an important role in the health of our planet. Forming the base of the ocean food chain, the billions of tiny algae that make up phytoplankton supply more oxygen to the planet's living organisms than the world's biggest tropical jungles. Marine forests, like sea grass beds, seaweed, and mangrove swamps, all help to protect the coast from erosion, waves, and currents. These underwater jungles provide a stable environment for small animals and serve as hiding places from predators.

Seaweed

There are 25,000 species of marine algae, often called seaweed. These plants have no stems, leaves, flowers, or roots. Like land plants, seaweed contains chlorophyll, a green coloring, that helps it absorb sunlight, which is needed to help it make oxygen and grow. While some types of seaweed float freely on the ocean's surface, others stick to rocks with the help of tiny suckers.

Mangrove swamps

Large forests of mangrove trees grow at the mouths of tropical rivers. These are the only trees that can grow in saltwater. Their roots, which rise up out of the water, are covered in thousands of small holes. These help the mangroves breathe, even though they are anchored in the underwater mud. One of the richest environments on the planet, mangrove swamps are unique places where monkeys, reptiles, fishes, and crustaceans live close together.

Kelp forests and sea otters

Kelp refers to a group of giant brown seaweeds that form large jungles in temperate water. Kelp forests are home to sea otters, which feed on them, raise their families in them, and even sleep tangled up in them!

Sea grass beds
Large underwater prairies of sea grass can be found growing in calm, clear, shallow water. Unlike seaweed, sea grass has roots that anchor in the mud and flowers that bloom underwater. It grows to about 4 ft (1.2 m) in height. Sea grass beds serve as shelter for rare animals like the dugong, a grass-eating marine mammal.

An unusual climber
With the help of its fins that work like legs, the mudskipper can leave the water and climb into mangrove trees to swallow insects! This fish can move more quickly on land than in water. It carries a supply of water in its mouth to help it breathe when it goes for a walk.

A good shot
The archerfish lives in the mangroves, where it feeds on insects. With perfect aim, it can spit a small stream of water on an insect sitting on a mangrove tree. Knocked off balance, the insect falls into the water, where it is swallowed by the fish.

The longest weed
Giant kelp is a type of seaweed that grows in cold coastal waters such as those found off California. Giant kelp can measure 200 ft (60 m) in length—equivalent to an 18-story skyscraper! Besides being the longest seaweed in the world, it is also the fastest-growing plant. Giant kelp, in fact, can grow 1 to 2 ft (30 to 60 cm) per day, which means you can almost see it growing before your eyes!

The conquest of the oceans

From the very beginning, human beings have searched the oceans for food and treasures of all kinds. With the help of improving technology, humans have managed to venture both farther out and deeper to collect what they need. Although we continue to benefit from the many riches the ocean provides us, its resources are slowly being reduced because of excessive fishing and pollution.

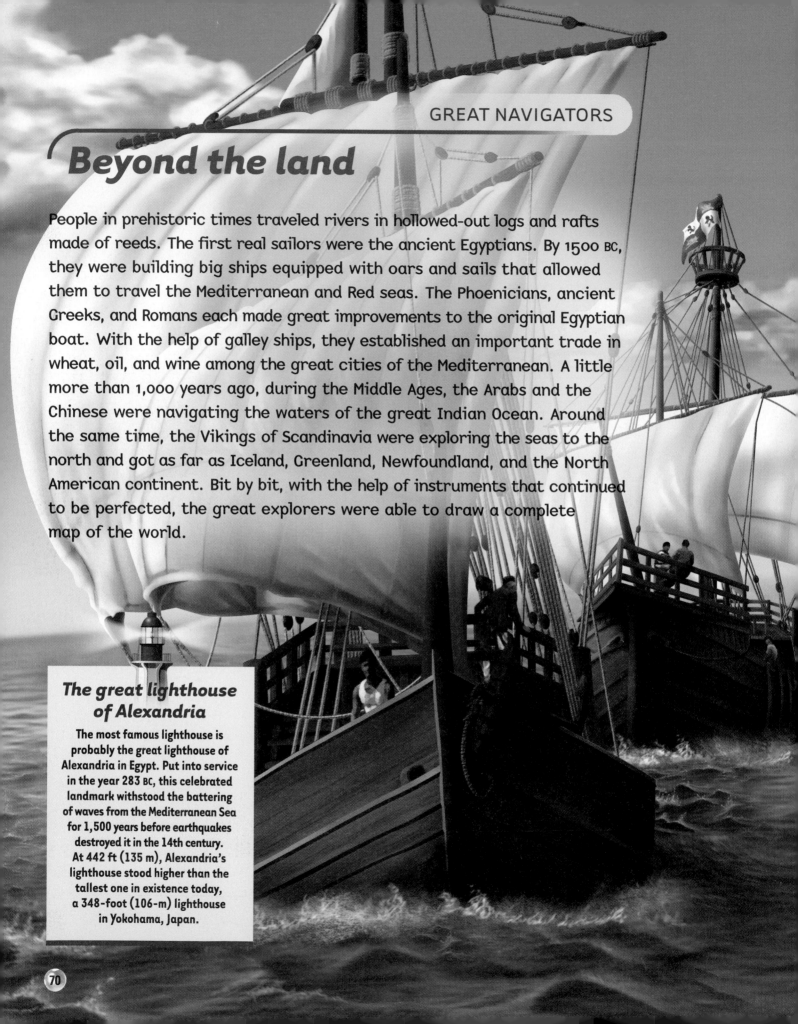

Beyond the land

People in prehistoric times traveled rivers in hollowed-out logs and rafts made of reeds. The first real sailors were the ancient Egyptians. By 1500 BC, they were building big ships equipped with oars and sails that allowed them to travel the Mediterranean and Red seas. The Phoenicians, ancient Greeks, and Romans each made great improvements to the original Egyptian boat. With the help of galley ships, they established an important trade in wheat, oil, and wine among the great cities of the Mediterranean. A little more than 1,000 years ago, during the Middle Ages, the Arabs and the Chinese were navigating the waters of the great Indian Ocean. Around the same time, the Vikings of Scandinavia were exploring the seas to the north and got as far as Iceland, Greenland, Newfoundland, and the North American continent. Bit by bit, with the help of instruments that continued to be perfected, the great explorers were able to draw a complete map of the world.

The great lighthouse of Alexandria

The most famous lighthouse is probably the great lighthouse of Alexandria in Egypt. Put into service in the year 283 BC, this celebrated landmark withstood the battering of waves from the Mediterranean Sea for 1,500 years before earthquakes destroyed it in the 14th century. At 442 ft (135 m), Alexandria's lighthouse stood higher than the tallest one in existence today, a 348-foot (106-m) lighthouse in Yokohama, Japan.

THE ROUTES OF THE GREAT EXPLORERS

In the 15th century, Europeans were in search of maritime routes to the riches of India and China: silk, spices, jewels, and gold. Portuguese explorer Vasco da Gama established the first spice route, sailing eastward around Africa to India in 1497 and 1498. Between 1492 and 1504, Italian navigator Christopher Columbus headed west, following currents that took him to the West Indies. From 1499 to 1502, Italian sailor Amerigo Vespucci explored the coast of Brazil and gave his name to the new continent: America. In 1522, the ship of Portuguese explorer Ferdinand Magellan completed the first voyage around the world. Between 1768 and 1779, Englishman James Cook explored the Pacific islands of Australia, New Zealand, Hawaii, and New Caledonia.

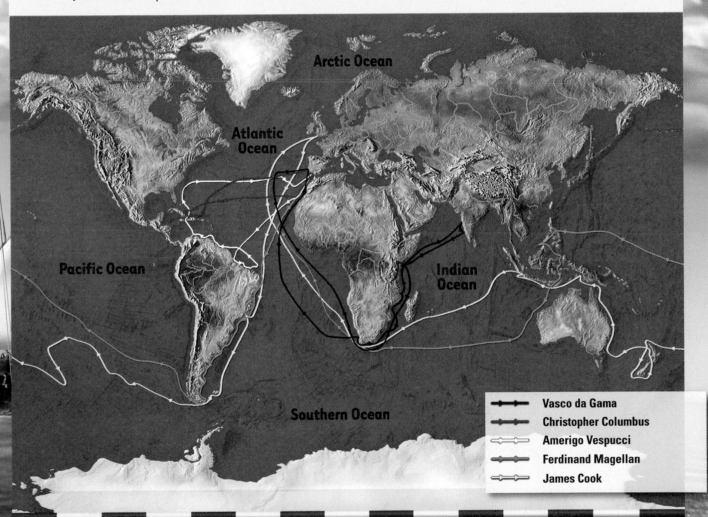

Arctic Ocean

Atlantic Ocean

Pacific Ocean

Indian Ocean

Southern Ocean

►—●—►	Vasco da Gama
►—◆—►	Christopher Columbus
▻—◇—▻	Amerigo Vespucci
►—◆—►	Ferdinand Magellan
▻—◇—▻	James Cook

Instruments

The invention of navigational instruments allowed early sailors to travel farther than they ever had before. The compass, invented by the Chinese more than 2,000 years ago, was commonly used around the year 1000. It helped navigators locate north at any time. The marine astrolabe, which appeared in the 15th century, allowed them to calculate latitude, which is the ship's northern or southern position in relation to the equator. The marine chronometer, which came along in 1735, helped navigators determine their longitude, which is the ship's eastern or western position. Finally, the sextant, which came into use in the 18th century, allowed sailors to calculate their position even more precisely than before.

The ocean's mysteries uncovered

For thousands of years, humans have combed the ocean floor for food, shells, pearls, and treasures hidden away in shipwrecks. As long ago as 4500 BC, the Mesopotamians, living in what is now Iraq, gathered mollusks from the bottom of the sea. The Mesopotamians held their breath for up to four minutes at a time and were able to dive 33 feet (10 m) below the surface of the water. Going any deeper than this is dangerous without special equipment. In 1690, English scientist Edmund Halley invented a wooden diving bell that allowed a person to descend even farther—to a depth of 59 feet (18 m) and remain there for more than an hour. Fresh air was fed into the bell by a hose that was connected to the surface. The waterproof deep-sea suits of today allow divers to descend to a depth of nearly 1,970 feet (600 m). With the help of underwater vehicles and robots, humans are now able to explore some of the deepest places on Earth, around 36,000 feet (11,000 m) beneath the surface.

The *Challenger* expedition

Between 1872 and 1876, the ship HMS *Challenger* sailed 79,277 miles (127,584 km) across the Atlantic, Pacific, and Indian oceans. Its mission was to estimate how deep the oceans were and to learn more about what is hidden in them. The temperatures, currents, salt levels, and depths were measured in different places, while samples of marine life and sediment were collected. This great expedition collected far more information about the oceans than any before it. There were 4,417 new species of marine life identified, and the existence of long underwater mountain ranges and deep ocean trenches was discovered. The *Challenger* expedition marked the beginning of oceanography, the science that studies the oceans.

Into the deepest place in the world

In 1960, on board the bathyscaphe *Trieste*, Don Walsh and Jacques Piccard reached a spot in the Mariana Trench that was 35,813 ft (10,916 m) beneath the surface. After a descent that lasted almost five hours, the *Trieste* stayed there for 20 minutes. The bathyscaphe was able to withstand the water's crushing pressure. This diving record has never been equaled in more than 40 years!

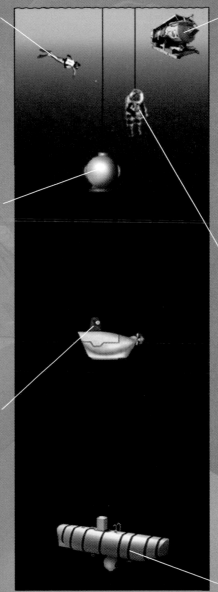

In 1943, Jacques Cousteau and Emile Gagnan invent the Aqua-Lung (nowadays called the scuba), an underwater breathing device equipped with a bottle of compressed air. For the first time, divers can move about freely and closely follow the movements of marine life to a depth of about 200 ft (60 m).

In 1934, William Beebe and Otis Barton invent the bathysphere, an underwater steel bubble connected by a cable to the surface. The two men descend to 3,028 ft (923 m) and become the first humans to observe deep-sea marine life in their natural habitat.

Active since 1964, *Alvin* is the first completely mobile vehicle able to transport passengers underwater, descending as deep as 14,764 ft (4,500 m).

In operation since 1993, *Aquarius* is the only undersea laboratory in the world. Lying off the Florida coast at a depth of 66 ft (20 m), *Aquarius* can accommodate six researchers. The lab is equipped with bunk beds, a shower, a toilet, a microwave oven, and a fridge.

The Jim suit is used in scientific, military, and commercial deep-sea expeditions. It allows a diver to descend to 1,970 ft (600 m). Any dive beyond such a depth requires an underwater vehicle.

Built to withstand the crushing pressure that exists at extreme depths, the bathyscaphes of the 1950s are the first underwater vehicles that can travel under their own power. Although bathyscaphes can move up and down, similar to an elevator, their ability to travel sideways is limited.

Observing the oceans

Scientists have come up with a variety of creative instruments for exploring the undersea world and reducing the dangers of navigation. Satellites in space survey the oceans from high above. They collect information about surface temperatures and currents, wave height, and the path of tropical storms. On board ships, radar sends out special radio waves that can detect obstacles like islands, coastlines, and other boats. The signals sent out by sonar equipment on boats travel underwater and show the depth and features of the ocean floor. Buoys are positioned at various depths in the ocean. They gather information on water temperature, pressure, and bottom currents. In the deepest areas, robots equipped with video cameras and moveable arms explore places that are difficult to get to. Large amounts of data are collected by all these instruments, which are linked to computers. Put together, this information allows scientists to recreate a virtual ocean. In the end, however, none of these sophisticated instruments will ever replace the human eye, which can observe the ocean directly through the window of a diving mask or an underwater vehicle.

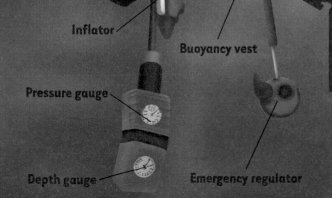

Regulator

Air tank

Mask

Video camera

Diving watch

Inflator

Buoyancy vest

Pressure gauge

Depth gauge

Emergency regulator

Scuba diver

With flippers, a mask, and a special suit to conserve body heat, a scuba diver makes his entry into the water. The diver deflates or inflates his buoyancy vest to help him balance at any depth. The air tank attached to the diver's back has a regulator, which controls the flow of oxygen through a tube to the diver's mouth. A pressure gauge shows the amount of air left in the tank, a depth gauge monitors how deep the diver is, and a special watch keeps track of how much time the diver has spent underwater.

Submersibles, or submarines, are vehicles designed for traveling underwater. The first submarines were used for military purposes. Today they are also used for scientific exploration. All submersibles dive and return to the surface using ballast tanks, which are compartments that can be filled with either air or water. When the ballast tanks are filled with water, the submarine becomes heavy and descends to the bottom. When the ballast tanks are filled with air, the submarine becomes lighter and rises to the surface.

Radio and antenna
The radio and the antenna are used to communicate with the outside world. They also help to pinpoint the submarine's location, which can be calculated to within a few feet (m).

Periscope
The periscope is a long tube with lenses and mirrors. It is used for scanning the ocean surface while the submarine remains hidden underwater.

Rudder
The rudder controls the submarine's left and right turns.

Diving planes
Diving planes control the rise and descent of the submarine and help it to remain stable while navigating underwater.

Wet suit

Flipper

A breathtaking record

The biggest submarines in the world can accommodate more than 160 crew members for a few months at a time—without ever surfacing! These giants measure about 564 ft (172 m) in length and they are almost as long as a football stadium.

75

The centuries covered up

Ancient cities and countless shipwrecks are spread over the ocean floor. Hidden under layers of sediment or overgrown with plants, coral, and sponges, these abandoned sites become home to a variety of marine animals. They also represent moments frozen in time, giving us a unique view of the civilizations that came before us. The statues, cannons, pottery, gold, silver, and leather garments preserved underwater attract not only treasure hunters, but scientists and historians, too. Thanks to the hard work of these experts, we can learn much about how our ancestors lived.

A famous wreck
On April 14, 1912, the world's largest ocean liner, the *Titanic*, hit an iceberg and sank near the coast of Newfoundland. Out of the approximately 2,228 people on board, only 705 survived. In 1985, 73 years after the sinking, a French and American expedition located the *Titanic*, resting on the ocean floor at a depth of 12,460 ft (3,798 m). Since then, robots and submersibles have brought up thousands of objects gathered from the wreck.

Techniques for uncovering the past

Shipwrecks can be located with the help of high-technology equipment like sonar. Robots or submersibles with lights, cameras, and moveable arms move in to get a closer look. The sediment is carefully removed using a large vacuum cleaner. Scientists photograph the wreck and make drawings of it on plastic sheets using wax crayons. This helps them chart the exact placement of every object found on the site. These objects are brought to the surface using ropes, floats, and sometimes cranes. Then they are numbered and labeled. Finally, they undergo a special treatment process to prevent damage by exposure to the air.

A chilling coincidence

Fourteen years before the sinking of the *Titanic*, writer Morgan Robertson published a novel that told the story of a huge ship hitting an iceberg in the North Atlantic. In Robertson's book, the accident takes place on a cold April night and the ship is named the *Titan*.

Food from the sea

With its plentiful supply of fish, crustaceans, mollusks, seaweed, and salt, the ocean has always been an important source of food for humans. Some coastal and island populations live almost entirely on what the sea can provide them, particularly fish. Today, more than 90 million tons of fish are caught worldwide. In the past, fishermen would bring their catch ashore right away, but today's fishing boats can remain at sea for months at a time. These fishing vessels are actually floating factories that clean, freeze, and pack or can the fish on the spot. Some ships are able to turn out 300,000 cans of fish in a day. To keep these factories busy, huge nets are spread out to scoop up entire schools of fish. While fishing techniques like these are extremely efficient, they can threaten the survival of some species. The nets may also accidentally trap seabirds, turtles, seals, and dolphins, which die by drowning.

A dangerous dish

A fugu, a kind of blowfish, contains enough poison to kill 30 people. Considered a delicacy in Japan, a plate of this fish may cost as much as $200! Chefs take a special course to learn how to prepare fugu and to remove its poisonous parts. Nevertheless, every year more than 100 people die after eating fugu that is improperly prepared.

Harvesting salt
Human-made salt flats are used to extract salt from the ocean. A system of canals directs the saltwater into a series of ponds that become less and less deep. Heated by the sun, the water evaporates as it passes from one pond to the next until, at the end, there is nothing left but salt crystals. About 66 million tons of salt are collected annually in this way.

Marine farming

Many marine animals are grown in captivity in coastal waters. They are kept in pens like farm animals. Most oysters and mussels eaten by humans are raised in baskets, on ropes, or on wooden poles specially set up for them. The business of breeding shrimp in captivity is booming, and the number of fish farms is on the rise. In fact, one out of every four fish eaten today was raised on a marine farm. While marine farms help prevent wild fish populations from shrinking, they can also destroy coastal ecosystems. Forests of mangroves have been torn down to install pens for raising shrimp or fish.

Seaweed farming

Seaweed is grown on large nets that are suspended in shallow coastal water. Seaweed is edible and is very rich in vitamins. It is also harvested to feed farm animals and is used to manufacture ice cream, toothpaste, medicines, fertilizer, and cosmetics.

Underwater riches

The ocean is a hiding place for many of the world's treasures. If it were possible to recover all the gold lost in the world's oceans, there would be enough to make a 5-pound (2.3-kg) gold bar for every person on Earth. Other treasures like coral, pearls, and seashells have been collected since the beginning of civilization and used as jewelry, money, decorations, and containers. We attach great value to these ocean resources, but often forget that they come from living organisms. Collecting too many of the ocean's natural treasures threatens their survival.

Univalve

Sponges

A sponge's skeleton has the remarkable ability to hold a lot of water. Sponges have been used for bathing and cleaning for thousands of years. The soldiers of ancient Rome quenched their thirst with water-soaked sponges they carried with them. Today, the manufacture of synthetic sponges has helped prevent a shortage of natural sponges.

Nodules

Nodules are large black pebbles that contain valuable metals like manganese, iron, copper, and nickel. There are an estimated 500 billion tons of nodules scattered on the ocean floor, lying about 13,000 to 20,000 ft (4,000 to 6,000 m) deep. In the Pacific Ocean, there is a field of nodules almost as big as Alaska!

Soft coral

People have been collecting soft coral since prehistoric times. This coral, used in jewelry, looks like tiny branches when it's in the water, and the most valuable kind is red. Found near the coasts of Asia and in the Mediterranean Sea up to 1,000 feet (300 m) deep, soft coral is rare today. Collectors must go even deeper to find it, and so much has been taken that it is in danger of disappearing.

Monster seashell

The giant clam lives near coral reefs. It measures more than 4 ft (1.2 m) across, weighs over 500 lbs (225 kg), and has the largest shell in the world. According to legend, the giant clam can trap an unsuspecting diver inside its shell. In reality, however, this creature is nothing more than a seaweed-eating vegetarian.

Shells

Shaped like spirals, fans, and butterflies, the shells we see scattered along the coast are the outside skeletons of mollusks. These creatures make their own shells out of a fluid they secrete that hardens into various shapes. A univalve mollusk, such as the periwinkle, has only one shell, while a bivalve like the clam has two shells connected by muscle.

Bivalve

Pearls

Pearls are made by pearl oysters, which live in tropical oceans. The small, round, precious stones are formed when a foreign particle, such as a grain of sand, slips inside the shell of a pearl oyster. This creature secretes a substance called mother-of-pearl, which coats the grain of sand to prevent it from scratching the oyster's insides. Over time, many layers of mother-of-pearl build up around the grain of sand, creating a pearl.

An ocean of energy

About one-third of the world's crude oil and natural gas comes from deposits found below the ocean floor. They were formed millions of years ago by decaying plankton buried under the sediment. Gas and oil are essential to our daily lives. They make our vehicles run and help generate electricity. To extract these precious underwater deposits, large drilling platforms are set up in the ocean. Some of them are like floating towns that can accommodate about 100 workers for several weeks at a time. The platforms are designed to withstand waves of more than 100 feet (30 m) in height and winds of 140 miles per hour (225 km/h) as well as tsunamis, earthquakes, and fires. The most productive platforms, located in the North Sea, the Gulf of Mexico, and the Persian Gulf, extract millions of barrels of crude oil each day.

Drilling

Crude oil deposits may lie several thousand feet (m) below the ocean floor. To reach them, a well must be dug into the seabed from the drilling platform. A rotating drill bit at the end of a long tube bores through the undersea rock until it reaches the deposit. The oil is pumped up to the platform, and an oil tanker or underwater pipeline brings it to shore.

The energy of the future
Our use of oil and natural gas is greatly polluting the environment, and our supply of these resources is running out. To face the growing demand for more energy, engineers are turning to nonpolluting and renewable energy sources. Already, there are power stations using the movement of the ocean's tides to run turbines that produce electricity. Currents and waves could also be put to use. Huge wind turbines have been set up along coastal areas to generate electricity by using the power of offshore winds.

Wind turbine

A skyscraper in the water

One of the tallest drilling platforms in the world is located in the Gulf of Mexico off the coast of Louisiana. It rises from the sea bottom, 2,860 ft (872 m) below the surface, and soars 420 ft (128 m) in the air. This drilling platform stands 3,280 ft (1,000 m) high and is taller than any skyscraper or tower found on dry land!

A sick ocean

For a long time, the ocean was treated like a giant garbage can that could make all our waste disappear. But the waste does not disappear. It pollutes the coastline and can drift for thousands of miles (kilometers), even as far as the poles. Almost half of the pollution in the ocean comes from land. Sewage, industrial waste, fertilizer, and chemical products used in farming are carried down rivers and out to sea. Nuclear waste in concrete containers is stockpiled at great depths. Any small crack in the concrete could cause an ecological disaster. Along the coast, both tourist and industrial developments destroy many natural habitats like mangrove swamps, sea grass beds, and coral reefs. Off shore, turtles are strangled by plastic bags that they mistake for jellyfish, birds become coated in crude oil, fish are poisoned, and dolphins are trapped in abandoned fishing nets.

Poison on our plates

Humans dump all kinds of poisons into the ocean, including dangerous metals like mercury and pesticides such as DDT (a chemical product used to kill insects). These toxic substances are absorbed by plankton. The marine creatures that feed on plankton are in turn contaminated. At each stage on the way up the food chain, the concentration of poison builds. Sea mammals, large fish, and human beings at the top of the chain may absorb amounts of toxic substances one million times more concentrated than the water originally contained. It has been discovered that exposure to these substances can cause serious diseases like cancer, brain damage, and birth defects.

Black tides

Thousands of tons of crude oil can be spilled in an oil tanker accident, causing a kind of pollution called a black tide. Black tides pollute coastlines, kill birds, and poison marine plants and animals. The thick layer of black oil on the ocean's surface prevents the Sun's rays from reaching into the water, affecting the algae and, in turn, the entire food chain. In 1989 the black tide caused by a spill from the oil tanker *Exxon Valdez* in Alaska was responsible for the deaths of 250,000 birds, 2,800 otters, 300 harbor seals, 250 bald eagles, and 22 killer whales.

Mercury contamination

Between 1932 and 1968, a factory spilled mercury into Minamata Bay in Japan. Over time this led to one of the worst human and environmental tragedies ever. Fish and shellfish were contaminated by the mercury. The local population ate the contaminated fish and were poisoned by the mercury. Hundreds of people died, including many children and newborns. Thousands of others became critically ill, and many were deformed or paralyzed for life.

Animals in peril

Every day, some of Earth's creatures disappear before anyone has even had a chance to discover or study them. Human beings are partly to blame. Pollution contaminates plants and animals, making them less resistant to disease and making it difficult for them to reproduce. Over time, their populations are reduced and they eventually disappear. Along coasts, buildings have overrun the natural habitats of animals, chasing them away. Industrialized fishing drives certain species to the edge of extinction. It is only recently that people have become aware of how fragile our oceans really are. Around the world, countries are creating laws that control fishing, limit pollution, and set aside areas that protect marine life. Today there are more than 1,000 marine sanctuaries, the largest being Australia's Great Barrier Reef.

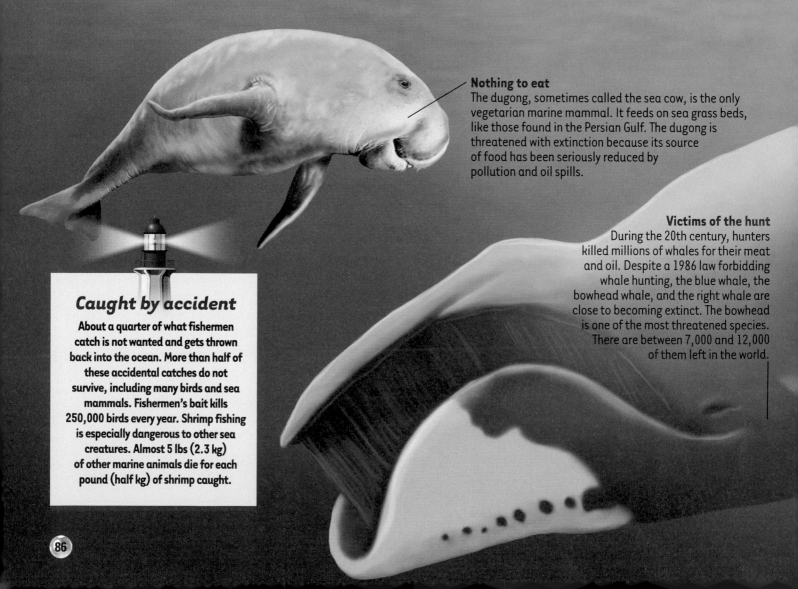

Nothing to eat
The dugong, sometimes called the sea cow, is the only vegetarian marine mammal. It feeds on sea grass beds, like those found in the Persian Gulf. The dugong is threatened with extinction because its source of food has been seriously reduced by pollution and oil spills.

Victims of the hunt
During the 20th century, hunters killed millions of whales for their meat and oil. Despite a 1986 law forbidding whale hunting, the blue whale, the bowhead whale, and the right whale are close to becoming extinct. The bowhead is one of the most threatened species. There are between 7,000 and 12,000 of them left in the world.

Caught by accident
About a quarter of what fishermen catch is not wanted and gets thrown back into the ocean. More than half of these accidental catches do not survive, including many birds and sea mammals. Fishermen's bait kills 250,000 birds every year. Shrimp fishing is especially dangerous to other sea creatures. Almost 5 lbs (2.3 kg) of other marine animals die for each pound (half kg) of shrimp caught.

Caught in a trap
Vaquitas are small porpoises that can only be found in Mexico's Gulf of California. The vaquita population is threatened by fishing and pollution, and it is estimated that there may be only about 500 of them left. Every year about 50 of these porpoises are strangled by fishing nets.

An extinct bird
The great auk, a large flightless seabird that once lived in the North Atlantic, has entirely disappeared. They were frequently hunted for their feathers and meat during the 16th and 17th centuries. No auks have been seen since 1844.

Disappearing seals
A few years ago, thousands of monk seals could be spotted around the Mediterranean seacoast. Today there are no more than 500 of them surviving in these polluted waters. The monk seal is one of the world's most threatened species.

Predators turned prey
Every year, humans kill 100 million sharks, either on purpose or by accident. Valued for their meat, sharks are ending up on people's plates. They are also being hunted down as trophies. Even the much-feared great white shark is paying the price for its bad reputation, and is now considered a vulnerable species.

Reefs at risk
According to recent studies, 58 percent of the world's coral reefs are in danger because of human activity and 25 percent have been destroyed or seriously damaged by global warming. Coral reefs suffer from a variety of illnesses such as coral bleaching, in which the reef turns white and eventually dies. This occurs when the tiny algae that live on the reefs are driven away because of global warming and pollution. Without the algae, the coral cannot survive.

Facts

MAIN FEATURES OF THE OCEAN FLOOR

Emperor Seamount

Kuril-Kamchatka Trench

Japan Trench

Mariana Trench

Philippines Trench

Aleutian Trench

Puerto Rico Trench

Java Trench

Peru-Chile Trench

Mid-Atlantic Ridge

Triple Indian Ridge

Kermadec-Tonga Trench

East-Pacific Rise

Famous maritime disasters

Claiming more than 1,500 victims, the sinking of the *Titanic* remains one of history's biggest maritime tragedies. Although other terrible accidents have occurred at sea, many seem to have been forgotten over time. Here are a few of them:

• On May 29, 1914, the Canadian ocean liner *Empress of Ireland* collides with a Norwegian coal carrier in thick fog on Canada's St. Lawrence River. The *Empress* sinks in 14 minutes, taking 1,012 passengers and crew members with it.

• On May 7, 1915, the liner *Lusitania*, used to transport goods and people between England and the United States, is torpedoed by a German submarine off the coast of Ireland. The death of almost 1,200 civilians shocks America, convincing the country to join the Allies in World War I.

• On January 30, 1945, during World War II, the German liner *Wilhelm Gustloff* is torpedoed by a Soviet submarine in the Baltic Sea. Between 6,000 and 7,000 German passengers and sailors on board the liner are killed.

• On December 3, 1948, the steamship *Kiangya*, overloaded with passengers, hits a mine off the coast of China. It sinks, killing 2,750 people.

• On December 20, 1987, off the coast of Manila in the Philippines, the ferryboat *Doña Paz* collides with an oil tanker. It is believed that as many as 4,340 passengers may have been killed.

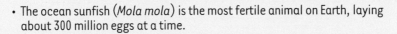

Marine animal records

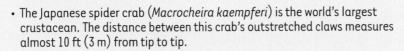

- The ocean sunfish (*Mola mola*) is the most fertile animal on Earth, laying about 300 million eggs at a time.

- The Japanese spider crab (*Macrocheira kaempferi*) is the world's largest crustacean. The distance between this crab's outstretched claws measures almost 10 ft (3 m) from tip to tip.

- The whale shark (*Rhincodon typus*) is the world's largest fish, measuring up to 50 ft (15 m) in length and weighing more than 10 tons. Despite its terrifying size, the whale shark is harmless and eats only plankton.

- The oarfish (*Regalecus glesne*) is the longest bony fish in the world. With its slim body that measures more than 26 ft (8 m) long and fins that resemble a red mane, this odd fish looks as if it belongs in a science fiction novel.

- The female sea worm Bonellia (*Bonellia viridis*) measures 3 ft (1 m) in length, but its partner is tiny. Barely 1/24 of an inch (1 mm) long, the male sea worm actually lives inside the female. This is the biggest difference in size between the sexes in the entire animal kingdom.

- The ocean quahog (*Arctica islandica*) is a kind of clam that can live 220 years. This mollusk holds the record for the longest-living animal in the world.

- The cuskeel (*Abyssobrotula galatheae*) is the deepest-living fish known. This creature measures about 8 in. (20 cm) in length and has been spotted at the bottom of the Puerto Rico Trench, about 27,500 ft (8,400 m) beneath the ocean's surface.

- The seahorse is the slowest-moving fish. It travels at a speed of about 3/8 of an inch (1 cm) per hour. The seahorse is also the only animal in which males, not females, give birth to their young.

- Mako sharks, dolphins, and killer whales are the ocean's high-jump champions. These animals are able to jump 20 to 23 ft (6 to 7 m) into the air—a record!

- The calls of the blue whale can measure as high as 188 decibels. Its sound is louder than that of a jumbo jet during take-off.

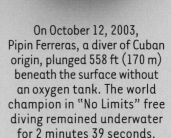

On October 12, 2003, Pipin Ferreras, a diver of Cuban origin, plunged 558 ft (170 m) beneath the surface without an oxygen tank. The world champion in "No Limits" free diving remained underwater for 2 minutes 39 seconds.

There are more species of fish than there are of mammals, birds, and reptiles combined.

Fish is a primary source of protein in the human diet. People around the world eat far more fish than beef and chicken.

Almost 6 people in 10 live in coastal areas less than 37 miles (60 km) from the ocean.

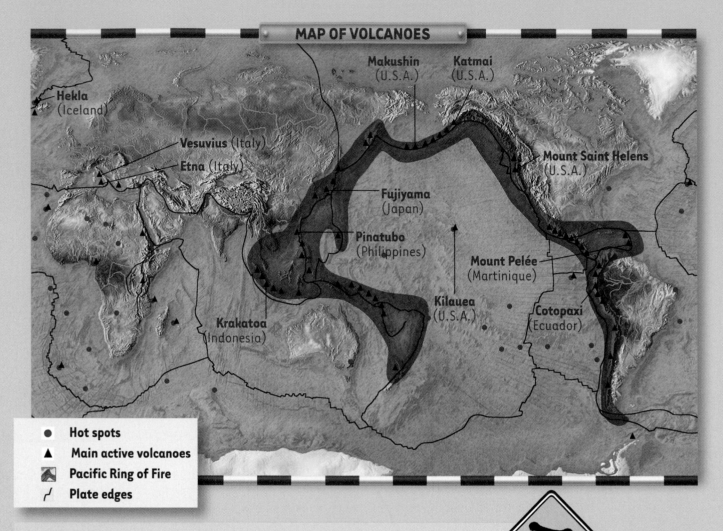

Hekla (Iceland)
Makushin (U.S.A.)
Katmai (U.S.A.)
Vesuvius (Italy)
Etna (Italy)
Mount Saint Helens (U.S.A.)
Fujiyama (Japan)
Pinatubo (Philippines)
Mount Pelée (Martinique)
Kilauea (U.S.A.)
Cotopaxi (Ecuador)
Krakatoa (Indonesia)

● **Hot spots**
▲ **Main active volcanoes**
Pacific Ring of Fire
Plate edges

Mortal danger

- The box jellyfish, commonly known as the sea wasp (*Chironex fleckeri*), is considered by many to be the most poisonous animal in the world. It lives in the waters of northern Australia and Southeast Asia. This creature's long tentacles contain powerful venom that can kill a person in anywhere from 30 seconds to 4 minutes.

- The sea snake *Hydrophis belcheri* lives in the Timor Sea off the coast of Australia. Its venom is 100 times more poisonous than that of any snake that lives on land. Luckily, this creature won't bite a human being unless it is provoked.

- The saltwater crocodile (*Crocodylus porosus*) is the largest reptile in the world. This ferocious beast lives in the waters off Asia and northern Australia and can measure up to 23 ft (7 m) in length. Saltwater crocodiles eat anything they come across, including human beings.

- Among the hundreds of species of sharks in the oceans, no more than 15 kinds are a threat to human beings. The great white shark, the tiger shark, and the bull shark are the most dangerous. These sharks do not go after people intentionally; when they do attack, it is often because they've mistaken a human for a marine animal. Since sharks do not especially like human flesh, they usually let go after the first bite.

The oceans are home to a great variety of organisms. Around 250,000 different kinds of organisms have been identified. Many more, perhaps millions, are still to be discovered.

MAP OF THE PRINCIPAL OCEAN CURRENTS

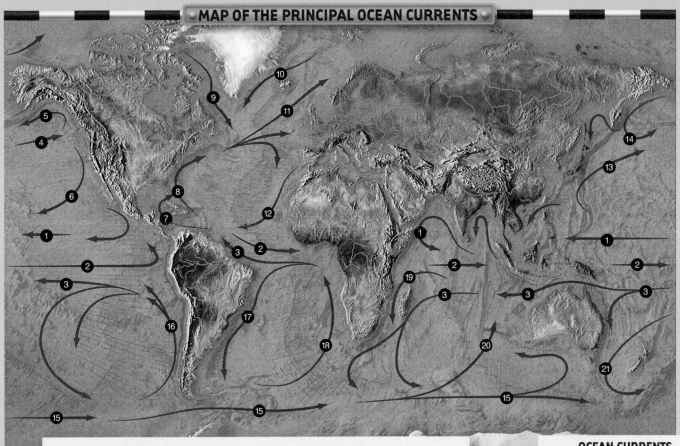

1. North Equatorial Current	12. Canary Current
2. Equatorial Countercurrent	13. Kuroshio
3. South Equatorial Current	14. Oyashio
4. North Pacific Drift	15. Antarctic Current
5. Alaska Current	16. Peru Current
6. California Current	17. Brazil Current
7. Caribbean Current	18. Benguela Current
8. Gulf Stream	19. Agulhas Current
9. Labrador Current	20. West Australia Current
10. Greenland Current	21. East Australia Current
11. North Atlantic Drift	

OCEAN CURRENTS

Warm

Cool

The port of Singapore is the busiest in the world. More than 142,000 ocean-going ships load and unload their cargo here each year. About 1,000 ships are tied to its docks at all times.

Field trip to the seacoast

The best time for observing the coast and its inhabitants is at low tide, when a large part of the shore is uncovered and waiting to be explored. Because the times of the tides change from one place to another and from one day to the next, check the local tide tables before you head out. You can usually find them posted in tourist areas. Ask your parents to help you.

To get the most out of your field trip to the seacoast, and to avoid injury, be sure to bring along the following:

- **Hat**
- **Non-slip shoes**
- **Magnifying glass**
- **Camera**
- **Sunscreen**
- **Binoculars**
- **Small shovel**
- **Pencil and notebook**

Important!

- **Never go for a walk by the sea without an adult to supervise you.**
- **Do not climb on slippery rocks or rocks covered in algae.**
- **Do not go near cliffs. Be on the lookout for the rising tide and big waves.**
- **Watch where you step.**
- **Do not touch living animals.**

CHECK THE ROCKS

Many animals protect themselves from the sun and the waves by clinging to the undersides of rocks. To observe these creatures, find a few large, damp rocks and lift them gently. You may discover mollusks, such as mussels and periwinkles, or even crustaceans, like barnacles and crabs. Always put the rock back exactly the way you found it.

OBSERVE THE SEAWEED

On rocky coasts, you can find seaweed clinging to rocks. Observe the weeds up close, without stepping on them. They are full of little air bubbles that help them float at high tide. Lift some seaweed gently with your shovel. Are there any animals hiding underneath?

DIG IN THE SAND

At first glance, sandy beaches may look deserted, but they are actually swarming with life. All you have to do is dig. Many animals are buried under the sand and have left their traces, such as air openings, on the surface. Find a hole and start digging next to it. You may find sea worms, or mollusks such as cockles and clams. After your observations, put the sand back the way it was.

EXAMINE THE PEBBLES

The pebbles you find on the seashore are often smooth and rounded. They have been polished by the continuous movement of the waves and by rubbing against sand and other pebbles.

Periwinkle

Seaweed

Barnacles

Crab

Mussel

Clam

Cockle

Make your own observation mask

The pools of water left by the high tide are full of life. Observing what lies inside these rock pools may be difficult, however, because of your reflection or the Sun's reflection on the water's surface. Here is how to make a mask that will let you see the world that lives below.

Materials needed

- A large milk or juice carton
- Plastic food wrap
- Waterproof adhesive tape
- Two large elastic bands
- Scissors

Experiment

1. Use the scissors to cut the top and bottom off the carton. Ask an adult to help you.

2. Tear off a piece of plastic food wrap that is large enough to completely cover one end of the carton as well as its four sides.

3. Use the adhesive tape to tape the edges of the plastic wrap to the carton.

4. Use the two elastic bands to hold the plastic wrap in place near each end of the carton.

How to use the mask

Bring your new observation mask on your next walk along the seaside. Set yourself up in a comfortable position next to a rock pool. Make sure it is a safe spot where you won't lose your balance. Place the end of the carton that is covered in plastic under the water's surface and look down through the carton from the other end. Without moving, observe the different forms of life in the water.

SEARCH FOR THE REMAINS OF MARINE ANIMALS

The seashells scattered on the shore come in many different forms. The shells of cockles are fan-shaped. Those of limpets are more cone-shaped. Whelks have large, spiral-shaped shells. The shells of periwinkles resemble those of snails. Look for other signs of life: the feathers of seabirds, the empty shells of crabs, and the skeletons of sea urchins or starfish.

Starfish

Whelk

Sea urchin

Limpet

WATCH THE BIRDS

Using your binoculars, watch the different seabirds that come to feed on the coast. Some, like cormorants, dive into the water to catch fish. Others, like gulls, look for shellfish. They pick them up in their beaks, fly into the sky, and drop them on the rocks. The shells break open and the gulls eat the shellfish.

Cormorant

Gull

WATCH THE ROCK POOLS

As the high tide recedes, it leaves behind large pools of water scattered along rocky coastlines. These natural aquariums are often shallow, and allow you to safely observe the aquatic environment they contain. You may discover live seaweed, sponges, starfish, crabs, sea anemones, and even small fish.

OBSERVE THE BITS OF WOOD

Pieces of dead wood washed up on the shore by the waves and tides hide living creatures. Crack open a piece of soft wood with your shovel. You may find shipworms, which are small mollusks that dig tunnels in wood. Observe the shipworms' long tunnels with your magnifying glass, then put the wood back where you found it.

BRING BACK SOUVENIRS

You can bring back souvenirs from your walk on the coast by taking notes and photographs and by making drawings of what you have seen. But never take anything that came from the shore. Remember that the shellfish, seaweeds, rocks, and pieces of wood all have a role to play on the coast. They may serve as food or provide a hiding place for a number of small creatures. Leave the shore the way you found it.

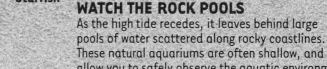

Glossary

A

Active volcano
A volcano that is erupting or likely to erupt in the future.

Amphibian
An animal that can live and breathe in water as well as on land.

Antarctic
The ice-covered continent situated at the southern end of Earth, including the South Pole.

Arctic
The land and seas situated at the northern end of Earth, including the North Pole.

Atmosphere
The layer of gases surrounding our planet.

C

Carapace
The hard shell that protects the bodies of some animals.

Climate
A pattern of weather common to a particular region of the planet. The pattern is determined by measurements taken over a long period of time.

Coastal region
An area bordering the ocean.

Colonization
The settling of a group of animals or humans in a new area.

Colony
A group of animals of the same species.

Concentration
A coming together of things or organisms in a limited area.

Crust
The hard layer covering Earth's surface.

Current
The movement of water in a specific direction.

D

Data
Information collected from research or by observation.

Debris
The remains of objects or organisms broken down or destroyed.

Decomposition
The process in which a dead plant or animal is rotting and crumbling apart.

E

Ecosystem
A natural environment in which different living organisms interact with one another.

Equator
An imaginary line that circles Earth midway between the two poles. It divides the planet into the Northern Hemisphere and the Southern Hemisphere.

Evaporation
The change from a liquid state into vapor.

Extinct
A species of animal or plant that no longer exists.

Extinct volcano
A volcano that is no longer likely to erupt.

G

Global warming
An increase in the average temperature on Earth from one year to the next.

H

Hemisphere
The northern or southern half of Earth. The two hemispheres are divided by the equator.

I

Ice floe
A large flat mass of floating sea ice commonly found in the polar regions.

Invertebrate
An animal that doesn't have a spinal column.

Islet
A small island.

L

Latitude
The northern or southern position of a place or an object in relation to the equator.

M

Microorganism
A tiny living organism that is only visible under a microscope.

Migration
Movement of a group of people or animals from one region to another.

Mythical
Imaginary people or places.

N

Nutrient
The food or chemical elements needed for an organism to live and grow.

P

Parasite
An organism that feeds off the inside or outside of another organism.

Pole
The poles represent either the northern or the southern end of an imaginary line or axis around which Earth seems to rotate.

Predator
An animal that hunts and eats other animals.

Pressure
The weight of water. In the ocean, the water pressure increases as one goes deeper because the amount of water above increases and weighs more.

Prey
Animals that are hunted and eaten by other animals.

R

Reef
Undersea rock or coral lying close to the surface of the water.

S

School
A group of fish of the same species.

Species
A group of animals or plants that are alike enough naturally that they can reproduce with one another.

Submersible
An underwater vehicle.

T

Tropics
The area of Earth around the equator where it is warm or hot all year. The tropics extend about 1,600 miles (2,575 km) north of the equator to the Tropic of Cancer and 1,600 miles (2,575 km) south of the equator to the Tropic of Capricorn.

V

Vegetation
A group of plants growing in an area.

Vertebrate
An animal that has a spinal column.

Index

Bold = Main entry

Index

Bold = Main entry